Reaching the Vulnerable Child

Delivering Recovery

Series edited by Patrick Tomlinson, Director of Practice Development, SACCS
This is an essential series on practice for all professionals and parents involved in providing recovery for traumatized children and young people. Each book offers a practical and insightful introduction to an aspect of SACCS' unique and integrated approach to children traumatized by sexual, physical and emotional abuse.

Reaching the
Vulnerable Child
Therapy with Traumatized Children

Janie Rymaszewska and Terry Philpot

Foreword by Mary Walsh

Jessica Kingsley Publishers
London and Philadelphia

First published in 2006
by Jessica Kingsley Publishers
116 Pentonville Road
London N1 9JB, UK
and
400 Market Street, Suite 400
Philadelphia, PA 19106, USA

www.jkp.com

Library of Congress Cataloging in Publication Data
Rymaszewska, Janie.
  Reaching the vulnerable child : therapy with traumatized children /
Janie Rymaszewska and Terry Philpot ; foreword by Mary Walsh.
    p. ; cm.
  Includes bibliographical references and index.
  ISBN-13: 978-1-84310-329-5 (pbk. : alk. paper)
  ISBN-10: 1-84310-329-X (pbk. : alk. paper)
  1. Abused children--Rehabilitation. 2. Child psychotherapy.
I. Philpot, Terry. II. Title.
  [DNLM: 1. Child Abuse--therapy. 2. Child Abuse--psychology.
3. Psychotherapy--methods--Child.   WS 350.2 R995r 2006]
RJ507.A29R93 2006
618.92'858223--dc22

                                                              2005032089

British Library Cataloguing in Publication Data
A CIP catalogue record for this book is available from the British Library

ISBN-13: 978 1 84310 329 5
ISBN-10: 1 84310 329 X

Printed and bound in Great Britain by
Athenaeum Press, Gateshead, Tyne and Wear

To Ismay for her unconditional belief in me.

Janie Rymaszewska

For Anne and John Dossett-Davies for friendship, delicious food,
the delights of Oxford and Oxfordshire, the arcana
of east European monarchies and much else.

Terry Philpot

Contents

Foreword

Following a dream of helping children who had been sexually abused to communicate about their distress and recover from it, Madge Bray and I started SACCS in 1987. We pioneered techniques to enable children to communicate using their own language, which for most of them is play. We used a specially designed toy box with carefully chosen play material, and saw children all over the country, representing them in courts and in other decision-making arenas, listening to their distress and helping them to have a voice. As our experience broadened, we became committed to helping them recover, and as the window of opportunity we have for recovery work is quite small, we have to take advantage of it.

Since then we have developed a range of services to meet the needs of this very vulnerable group of children, many of whom are emotionally fragmented. They are children who, because of their abusive experiences, have suffered profound harm, have attachment disorders, and have suffered multiple placement breakdowns and further abuse through the system. Because of this, both their internal and external worlds have been affected, and we recognize the need to help the whole child to recover, both in residential care and in family placement. There are three integrated strands to this important work: therapeutic parenting, life story work and therapy. This book is about therapy, but because of the integrated nature of the work, Janie Rymaszewska and Terry Philpot have set the context by describing the other two strands and making reference to them throughout.

Therapy has been integral to SACCS from the beginning, when we travelled the country providing our Sexual Abuse Child Consultancy Service, to the establishment of its first base in Shropshire, where the main office remains today.

The authors describe in some detail the uses of the box technique that Madge Bray and I developed in the early days. Our colleagues Pauline Flavin and Barbara Jones joined SACCS and helped to pioneer the work during the early stages, while Tony Baker, a consultant psychiatrist, helped to develop the SACCS approach to therapeutic work with these damaged children.

Through careful and sensitive work the therapist, always working at the child's pace, builds a relationship where the child can begin to explore her inner world, and slowly examine some of the harmful experiences in the past. The therapist begins to unravel the confused and overwhelming feelings the child has been trying to manage, and to externalize them so they no longer have the same power over her.

The child will then be able to reprocess her experiences, this time at her current age, with the therapist's help addressing distortions in her thinking, and gradually putting the past into some kind of perspective. This work is done in tandem with the life story work so that the child's history is clearly understood, without which the opportunity to address distortions would be impossible. The therapeutic parenting team provide the secure base from which this work can happen, and fill gaps in the provision of nurture and attachment of which these children have been so severely deprived.

Janie Rymaszewska and Terry Philpot have described the therapy, looking at how trauma affects the baby's developing brain and ability to form attachments, how therapy works in an integrated setting, dilemmas for the therapist, and case material, together with a general discussion of how therapy works.

We believe that every child who, through no fault of her own, has suffered abuse at the hands of an adult should have the opportunity to recover from her emotional injuries. Our hope is that this book will be a resource for all those working with these children therapeutically, and a reference for social workers, carers and other professionals.

The child's recovery belongs to her. This is a long and painful journey, and I never fail to be amazed at the courage of the children in undertaking it. We respect unconditionally the child's process, and we believe in keeping the child at the centre of everything that we do. Nowhere is this more important than in therapy.

Mary Walsh
Co-founder and Chief Executive, SACCS

Preface

Reaching the Vulnerable Child, the second book in the Delivering Recovery series, is intended for professionals who offer therapy that contributes to recovery from childhood trauma. It seeks to demonstrate how therapy forms a part of integrated treatment for recovery work and how therapists can tackle the complexities and paradoxes that are the direct result of traumatic early experiences. It is intended as an introduction and, like other books in the series, draws on insights gained from the work of SACCS but which have a wider application than just one agency.

Critical to explaining the therapy used (indeed, we would argue, critical to its success) is that therapy is a strategic part of an integrated treatment for recovery work. We show how therapists tackle the complexities and paradoxes that are the direct result of traumatic early experiences. The professional 'family' who make up the recovery team are, in time, perceived by the child to be safe; once trust is established, the child can then experience the commitment of her team to withstand a bombardment of her acting-out behaviours. She can then experience being contained in a robust yet caring way, and, thereby, is offered the opportunity to begin to accept help and support, to challenge her current behaviours. When a child reaches this point, there is the opportunity to gradually change the way she perceives herself and the world. The crucial role of therapy is to provide what Winnicott (1971) called the 'potential space' (the creative relationship between child and therapist) for every child gradually to explore her past experiences, within the safety and containment of metaphor, unless the child is too profoundly damaged by her past experiences to do so.

It is perhaps tempting (and more comfortable) for readers to envisage a child or adolescent having been successfully navigated through the various agencies that exist to bring a perpetrator to justice and the child to have been freed from her trauma; to imagine that this closes the case and, with time and support, that the child may even make a recovery; that she may be able to forget – albeit never forgive – and can move on to a new life.

How a child or adolescent arrives at this state of emotional repair is open to much scrutiny, and new approaches to trauma work are being rigorously researched. Yet the reality can be very different. It is more commonly the case that the child didn't want to be literally removed; she simply wanted the abuse to stop. She may be frightened and angry and feel traumatized by the rupture she experiences now that she no longer lives in the family home. She may desperately look for someone to blame and project her fury and impotence onto.

Perhaps this goes some way to explain the feelings of uneasiness that are evoked by these displaced children. Perhaps one begins to gain insights about the children when one realizes that it is a cluster of many of these emotions that drives these children on to find the physical and emotional energy to lash out at adults. It is why spending a day with these highly anxious children physically exhausts and emotionally drains those who are trying to get closer to them.

The approach we describe is in sharp contrast to previous placements which the child will have experienced: the recovery team provides containment and will work with the child to help her find different and more creative ways of ventilating her pain and outrage. Even if she were to lash out, the team will endeavour to re-frame the emotions that propelled her behaviour or acting out, and work with her to find a resolution. There is a commitment to withstanding the heightened anxieties and primitive panic that spurs the child into trying to push away the emotional help she so desperately needs.

The therapy outlined here is tailored to the individual needs of each child but holds to the basic assumption that therapist and child work together to try to make sense of her past experiences. The therapist works with the space between the inner and the outer world of the child as unconscious images may emerge in symbolic form. He will also be seeking to discover how the child has defended herself in order to survive each of the emotional, physical and sexual assaults as they impacted on her body and developing brain.

Keeping children safe

Keeping children safe and removing them, when necessary, from those who have harmed, or who might harm them, is the task of thousands of those charged with child protection working in social services departments, the NHS, education and the police.

When a child is taken into care, the task most commonly then becomes one whereby she is found a new foster or adoptive family. Legislation like the Adoption and Children Act 2002 and the Children Act 2004 is evidence of the priority that government has given to this, while regulations, guidance, performance indicators, and actions arising from inquiries into child deaths are also among the measures used to ensure that better services are provided to protect children.

However, too many children who have been damaged by their experiences at the hands of others pass from an unsafe environment to a physically safe one without what should be the necessary bridge on that journey, a means of moving from an abusive life to a satisfactory new one, from hurt to recovery. As Alice Miller (1995) writes: 'The damage done to us in childhood cannot be undone because we cannot change anything in our past. We can, however, change our selves' (p.28). Too little account is taken of the emotional needs of children traumatized through abuse. The 'selves' of these children will not be 'changed' if they are denied treatment and their past is allowed to cast a shadow across their future. This is one reason why so many placements break down. Children who have been abused often display eroticized behaviour that foster carers can find difficult to deal with. Moving placements then exacerbates children's problems so that the very thing that placements seek – stability – is the very thing that is denied to the child.

Instability follows from the disorder provoked by the trauma suffered by the child. Sometimes she will replicate the very behaviour that was shown to her. Children who have been abused can become abusive to their own or other people's children, and be violent and sexually predatory. The task of instilling a sense of internal stability and order in the child is a skilled, difficult and professional one. Describing the therapist's role in this task is the purpose of this book.

A note on the writing of this book

Names used for children referred to in case studies are pseudonyms. For ease of reading we have referred to children as 'she' and therapists and other staff as 'he'. Parents are also referred to by the male gender unless there is specific reference to a mother.

Acknowledgements

We are grateful to Patrick Tomlinson, Director of Practice, SACCS, for his oversight as the book progressed and his many helpful comments and assistance, and to his colleague, Billy Pughe, Managing Director, SACCS Care Ltd, for supplying information on therapeutic parenting. We are also grateful to Liz Brayne, Samantha Stubbs and Lorraine Macleod, who are therapists at SACCS, and Carolyn Butler, Deputy Director, Training, and Pauline Flavin, Director, who contributed towards the case material. Thanks to Richard Rose for his support and suggestions for the exercises at the end of the chapters; and to Lesley Gould and John Baker for early discussions. Paul van Heeswyk, child psychotherapist, Bridget Leverton, play therapist and Rachel Melville-Thomas, child and adolescent psychotherapist, contributed through conversations. Ann Pugh supported Janie Rymaszewska's writing with her administrative skills, as well as her thoughtfulness and encouragement. Andrew Constable and Mary Walsh, respectively Managing Director and Chief Executive of SACCS, have supported the series of which this book is the second volume. We should also like to thank Stephen Jones, our editor at Jessica Kingsley Publishers, and his colleague Leonie Sloman for their patience, advice and assistance.

From Pain to Recovery

Therapy and the Integrated Model

According to Hunter (2001), the task of therapy is 'to help children whose faith in adults is slim, whose experience of adults is dire and whose cynicism is often entrenched and well founded. Therapists have to communicate in a way that might reach these individuals' (p.1). In this, the therapist is offering the crucial role of helping to provide what Winnicott (1971) called 'potential space' for every child gradually to explore their past experiences, within the safety and containment of metaphor, unless the child is too profoundly damaged by her past experiences to do so. If this were the case, the therapist would have to adapt his therapy style to work more directly.

In the words of Hunter (2001), therapy is 'off to one side'. Therapists do not always work as part of a team, and even when they do, they may feel detached from other professionals because of their obligation to keep information that the child discloses confidential. Yet, as Siegel (2003) says:

> Therapy begins with connections. Filled with the heroism of a journey into the unknown, patients join with therapists in exploring the past, living fully in the present, and becoming the creative authors of the future chapters of their lives. Connections then

emerge beyond the therapeutic dyad, freeing the patient to explore new avenues of authentic living within the mind and with others. By making sense of our lives, we become free to join with others in creating emerging layers of meaning and connection. (p.8)

Children's lives are not compartmentalized, and thus therapy is not something set to be apart from their daily lives. For children receiving therapy, school, placement and many other matters have an impact upon them and may well feature in a therapy session. Thus, therapy cannot be 'off to one side'.

The basic task of the therapist is to facilitate the child's communication, verbally, non-verbally or symbolically, through play and the expressive arts, and to provide emotional containment so that she can move on emotionally, socially and educationally. Therapists working with traumatized children and young people should be aware of the potentially 'toxic' and 'hazardous' feelings that will need to be contained by them, before the child can feel safe enough to entrust to them her pain, rage and confusion. The primary task for the therapist is to build a relationship that is positive, warm and respectful, but at the same time able to withstand the bombardment of ambivalent feelings sure to arise within the therapy room, once the child is engaged in the therapy process.

A child brings what she wants to therapy. Children who have been traumatized require skilled and imaginative interventions if they are to achieve psychological and emotional health. A traumatized child is in emotional freefall. She has been separated from her parents, brothers and sisters and other family; she may have been through the criminal justice system; she is in the care of the local authority; she may have had placements that have broken down; and she may have incurred the hatred of her mother, her grandparents and her brothers and sisters. To such a child the recovery team offers a safety net. This specially constructed holding environment attempts to meet the needs of the traumatized child, who is without a secure anchor, who has lacked attachment and love and has experienced abuse, loss and separation.

With the integrated model, therapy is embedded in the recovery process. A child who is undergoing therapy will, at the same time, be experiencing therapeutic parenting and undertaking the journey that is life story work. The integrated model, which we describe below, takes as read what Hunter (2001) says: 'If [therapists] are to work effectively with accommodated young people, they have to take their place in the circle of people holding the safety net' (p.37).

The SACCS integrated model was developed through both experience and knowledge. Its three watchwords are *safety* (in place of fear); *containment* (in place of disintegration); and *attachment* (in place of detachment). It works with openness, not secrecy; communication, not avoidance; and predictability, not inconsistency.

How therapy fits into the integrated model

Within the therapeutic environment focused on recovery from trauma, a therapist needs to be prepared to adapt his technique and understand his impact on the residential setting as a whole, according to Wilson (1999). Unlike in a clinical outpatient setting, therapists cannot practise with the same degree of privacy or confidentiality. Customary procedures of establishing the boundaries of an individual psychotherapeutic setting need to be modified. In a residential setting, therapy is but one part of the overall therapeutic provision. As Wilson (1999) says: 'There is a danger that its privacy can be seen as secretive, arousing suspicion and envy, and having a generally divisive effect on the coherence of the community' (p.161).

Whereas confidentiality is important in individual psychotherapy, it is not something that can be absolute in a residential context. The recovery team need to know what is happening in the therapy session, particularly if, for example, a child becomes very upset as a result of allowing herself to engage in a session, and get in touch with powerful feelings. The emotional aftermath could trigger agitated or disruptive behaviour or sometimes self-destructive activity, for example suicide attempts, self-harming or absconding. The therapist will need to prepare the waiting carer to know that the child needs to be carefully supported on her return to the house or back to school.

In order to maximize the child's potential for recovery, confidentiality is held by the entire recovery team. In addition to the need for therapist and carers to inform each other of any anxieties they have about a child, the children themselves need to be aware that the adults will – and do – talk to each other. Children need to understand quite clearly that information about each of them is shared within the team. The child will eventually understand that this is the manner in which adults keep her safe, but it also ensures that the child does not split the team.[1]

Therapist and residential carer use different techniques and skills when working with a child. Within this setting it is important that, as well as sharing information and insights, they are able to respect each other's areas of expertise, and be clear about those boundaries. According to Cant (2002):

> The therapist's focus will inevitably be on the transference and the light that this throws on the deepest aspects of the child's internal world. They may work with the child's fantasies in a way that may not be available in the child's day-to-day experience in his home setting. (p.270)

Insights will be shared with carers or the life story worker to increase understanding of the child. It is acknowledged that the child will have a transference relationship to the therapist, her key carer and her life story worker. Each relationship forged by the child will be different. Therapists work with the transference – as do residential care workers – but this forms one of the key elements within therapy, as it informs the relationship between the two. Sometimes the child may indulge in a process called splitting – a defence mechanism – which typically involves attributing everything good to one person and everything bad to another person. Sometimes the therapist will be 'bad' and the care worker 'good' and vice versa. The child may try to draw either party into this thinking – sometimes to pit one against the other. Therapists are trained to be watchful of this process and if necessary, to share their observations with the child.

Important to the integrated way of working is the concept of special times, devised by Rachel Pinney. This evolved from a conviction by Pinney that children need to be listened to, that being heard and appreciated is essential for a child's growth. A child who receives a therapist's undivided attention will be allowed a chance to feel special where there is no ulterior motive, such as being groomed for an adult's sexual pleasure. The Children's Hours Trust (2002) describes special times or special hours as it is also called, as follows:

> The basic idea of special listening times for children is that children need regular periods of total attention from a caring adult. The adult supports and follows what the child is doing rather than making suggestions and imposing ideas. The adult uses neither praise nor blame...

In order to set in context the therapy described in this book, a short description is required of the two other elements of the integrated approach, as practised at SACCS: life story work and therapeutic parenting. While these will only be referred to in passing hereafter, it is necessary to bear in mind that a child who is undergoing therapy will, at the same time, be experiencing therapeutic parenting and undertaking life story work.

Life story work

Life story work was developed at SACCS. While life story work with children who are to be adopted is well established in social work, the life story work referred to here is richer, deeper, more detailed, takes considerably more time, and involves the child in gathering some of the evidence, telling her story, selecting materials to illustrate the story, and writing the story itself (Rose and Philpot 2004).

Life story work should furnish the answers to the questions What? Why? and When? about the child's life, but also Who? – who helped and who harmed the child? These answers allow children to express feelings about what they have experienced. It is a process (though here referring to life story work with children about to be adopted) that has been called 'unravelling confusion and discarding some of the negative emotional baggage which the child has carried for so long' (Connor *et al.* 1985).

Life story work attaches importance to the past. However, the past is seen, in this approach, as part of the therapeutic process, as much more than merely chronological or even factual. As Rose and Philpot (2004) ask:

> is the past about the relaying of facts and information alone or is it also about what the child believes the past to be, even though that may not be, in a strictly literal and factual sense, true? Life story work is about the people in the child's life, what happened to the child and the reasons why those things happened. It is not, and cannot be, a simple narrative or description. For example, recording that a child was moved from a foster care placement is less helpful than explaining why it happened, which means revealing to the child the real reasons, rather than those which may have been given at the time. (p.16)

The work, which from the preparatory stage to the final production of the life story book can take up to 18 months or 36 sessions, also involves much travel, visiting, research and interviewing. It requires interviewing people who have been part of the child's life from family to foster carers, social workers to abusers, residential workers to teachers. It involves reading social work and court reports; searching out official documents like birth, marriage and death certificates, and electoral registers; visiting (with the child) places where she has lived or which are significant (say, a holiday site); talking to the child at great length and liaising with her current carers (therapist, foster parents and residential workers); drawing up both family trees and ecomaps (diagrams placing the child in the middle with all the people associated with her panning out from her); as well as helping the child create her life story book.

Life story work is based on the belief that none of us can ignore what has happened in the past and then just move on. This is even more so with traumatized children, for the magnitude of their experiences can be so great that their past overshadows their present. The past must be faced, analysed, understood and, finally, accepted. Then progress, recovery, is possible.

Therapeutic parenting

The third and equally important part of the integrated model is therapeutic parenting. Children whose abuse was severe will have attachment problems because of interference with their emotional development (see Chapter 4). The response to this is to compensate for deficiencies in their parenting with a therapeutic regime that is accepting and containing. They are being 'reparented' because the structured help that they require gives as near as possible an approximation to the kind of positive parenting which they should have received. Therapeutic parenting is not only about the creation of a physical environment reminiscent of an ordinary home but is also the kind of care that the 'good' parent would have given to the child. It is the team of carers who work in the home who carry out the task of therapeutic parenting.

The majority of children who have been abused will not have received the emotional and physical nurture that is necessary for their development. This early privation or deprivation has left them with critical gaps in their emotional development; they may be left emotionally frozen or fragmented, and have an inner working model which severely impairs their ability to form healthy attachments.

As part of the integrated way of working, therapeutic parenting has been developed with the aim of providing a child with an experience of parenting that offers symbolic and actual experiences which seek to fill the gaps in her development. In time this provision will challenge the child's inner working model and enable her to begin to feel differently about herself, other people and the world around her.

An essential part of this work is the opportunity for the child to develop a primary attachment to one person, her key carer. It is through this primary attachment that the child will be able to experience a level of preoccupation, akin to maternal preoccupation normally associated with infancy, through which her recovery can take place. A key carer supported by the recovery team will ensure that all of the child's physical, emotional and therapeutic needs are met.

The environment where the child now lives is in itself a therapeutic opportunity and one that is psychically, as well as physically, significant. It is residential care that is non-institutional and specifically designed to meet the needs of the children. Every part of a child's life is seen as having therapeutic potential; therefore, the home is structured with great attention to the everyday details to reflect this.

For children who may have been deprived of so much, emotionally and physically, the home should have a sense of plenty being available: toys, games, art, ornaments, plants, furnishings, comics and books. The home should be child-centred and reflect the personalities and needs of the children who live there. At SACCS, the children live in small family-based homes for up to five children and a care team of ten, giving the children the opportunity to develop relationships within a protected environment.

Through internalizing their attachments and the experiences that they undergo in an accepting environment and with therapeutic parenting, the children are able to reach a level of recovery which enables them to move successfully on to family placement and achieve their potential.

CHAPTER 1

What is Sexual Abuse?

This book is about therapy with traumatized children who have been sexually abused, who have often also been physically abused and suffered from neglect. But what is sexual abuse and what do we know about it? The perception and definition of child abuse differs over time and cultures. For example, the degree of physical chastisement doled out by parents (and teachers) to children in the UK within living memory that was deemed perfectly acceptable, would today see the perpetrator before a criminal court.

By the same token, other forms of abuse towards children change according to the times and cultures in which they exist. In mid-Victorian England the age of consent was 14, and in some countries it is that today or even lower. For example, the age of consent in Chile and Mexico is 12; in Spain, North Korea and South Korea 13; and in Denmark, Sweden and France it is 15. In Northern Ireland, New York and Bolivia it is 17, while in California, Vietnam and Egypt it is 18, and in Tunisia 20 (*The Guardian* 2005). In some African and Middle East countries female genital circumcision is considered an acceptable practice, and, while it is illegal in the USA and the UK, operations are still carried out there. In some parts of India boys are masturbated to 'make them manly' and girls to 'make them sleep well'. In ancient Greece sexual relations between men and boys was accepted. Child prostitution in many countries is widespread, and this includes the United States, where there are said to be 300,000 child prostitutes, as well as more obvious places like Thailand where numbers are put at 200,000. Even in Britain there are thought to be 5000 children in the sex trade, whereas in France there are 8000 (Sanderson 2004). With the development of technology, the much easier dissemination and popularity of online pornographic images of children, which are also much more difficult to detect, feeds their exploitation in developing countries, as well as elsewhere.

Definitions of abuse have changed for many reasons, but much of it is to do with how definitions of childhood have changed, which itself is related, at least in part, to ideas about parenting and the responsibility and the relationship of parents to their children, both culturally and legally. So far as physical chastisement is concerned, the degree to which this can be administered has, over time, been influenced by what have been regarded as appropriate methods to deal with what adults have perceived as wrongdoing, as well as, in most recent times, the emerging concept of children's rights.[2]

This book is largely concerned with the effects upon children of sexual abuse, and the climate in which abuse takes place. Abuse normally occurs within a wider context of family dysfunction, privation and deprivation. Historically, it was neglect, rather than the other forms of abuse, which propelled three of the great children's charities – Barnardo's, the Children's Society and NCH – to come into existence, while the NSPCC was largely concerned with physical abuse and neglect.

There is some controversy about the extent of child abuse, partly occasioned by claims about how much goes unreported. Many people who have been abused reveal this only as adults, while many never reveal it at all.

The official figures show that 50–100 children die every year in the UK from abuse or neglect. They may not necessarily be on a local authority child protection register, but in March 2004 there were 26,3000 children and young people on such registers (this includes children who are categorized as 'children in need', and not all children on child protection registers are in care) (Department for Education and Skills 2005). There are 300,000–400,000 children in need; while three to four million children are judged as being 'vulnerable'. These figures are within a child population of 11 million (Department for Education and Skills cited in Revell 2003).

The Department of Health (2003) defined child sexual abuse in a way that commands general support, albeit emphases differ:

> Forcing or enticing a child or young person to take part in sexual activities whether or not the child is aware of what is happening. The activities may involve physical contact, including penetrative (eg, rape or buggery) and non-penetrative acts. They may include non-contact activities such as involving children in looking at, or in the production of pornographic material, or watching sexual activities, or encouraging children to behave in sexually inappropriate ways.

We might add to this the growing recognition that sexual abuse (or, at very least, collusion in sexual abuse) includes the buying, selling or otherwise disseminating and obtaining of pornographic videos, photographs, DVDs and films in which children, often no more than babies, feature. Thus, activities that may occur in a small town somewhere in the UK may be seen at the click of a button in the remotest parts of the United States or Russia.

Sexual activities involving children are many and varied and range, with regard to non-contact, from grooming children, insisting on sexually seductive behaviour and dress, to exposing a child to pornography and getting a child to recruit other children. With regard to contact this can go from open-mouth kissing and sexually arousing touching to rape, anal intercourse and oral sex. Sanderson (2004) offers a comprehensive list compiled from research into children's experiences. Nor is age respected by abusers: babies as well as 15-year-olds are sexually abused [3] The group estimated to be most at risk are children aged 5 to 12 years of age.

While sexual abuse, has always existed in all times and all societies, in the UK it is only in the last 25 or so years that it has come to prominence. Both boys and girls are sexually abused, but the greater number of cases involve girls by a ratio of nearly 4:1 according to one estimate (ChildLine 2003).[4] Children are most likely to be abused by someone they know, such as a family member or family friend, and this includes, of course, children who abuse other children. Abuse is also often systematic and continuing. It may last months or it may last years. Some children are abused into young adulthood, with the abuse only ending when they leave the family home, although even that is sometimes not the case. However, it tends to be abuse by strangers that can end in murder, and it is this that attracts front-page reporting. This has led to an over-emphasis on the concept of 'stranger-danger' in the media, which child protection agencies try to counter.

Just as sexual abuse has come to public and professional attention in comparatively recent times, so our understanding of its nuances continues to develop. As just mentioned, the idea of the predatory stranger while not a myth is, in reality, a rarity. The coming of the Internet has changed much about abuse, or rather it has allowed it to take new forms. It has made the dissemination of images both easier to do and much more difficult to detect: child pornography no longer has to be smuggled through customs when it can be sent through cyberspace by pressing a button. Rings of child abusers have also come to attention, but again a child is most likely to be introduced to one of these by a relative or someone she knows than by a stranger, and she may find in the ring, people whom she knows from her parent's or parents' acquaintance. While most abuse is perpetrated by men against girls, fathers can abuse sons, and mothers their daughters and sons. Couples can jointly abuse their children, while women can also collude in abuse when they do not actually commit it.

We now know much about the motivations of abusers and the effects of abuse, even if there is still much remaining to be learned.

CHAPTER 2

Blighted Lives, Hope Survives

A child who has been abused and is traumatized is first and foremost a child. It is important to strive always to see the child and not just the abuse. She is an ordinary child to whom extraordinary things have happened.

It is not possible to speak of a 'typical child' when it comes to describing the effects of abuse and trauma, because all children are different and react in different ways and the type of trauma varies greatly. However, it is possible to make some general statements about abused and traumatized children which are nevertheless illustrative.

Before we discuss these, it is important to remember that an abused child's perceptions of her abuse and other things may be very different from those who seek to help her. Alvarez (1992) explains this thus:

> What the abuse has meant for him [sic] and meant to him may be very different from its meaning for us. He may, for example, be too emotionally and cognitively blunted for anything much to have any meaning at all. Or he may have been corrupted himself and have become fascinated with abuse or an abuser himself. He may fear the abuser far more than he fears the abuse. Or he may feel deep love for the abusing figure and this love may be stronger than his fear or distaste for the abuse. Or he may have all of these difficulties. In any case, our notions of protection, of justice, of care, may be quite unreal to him. (p.152)

If this is the case, it is not difficult to imagine the desperate dilemma and double bind facing a young child who has disclosed abuse and is trying to make sense of the new chaos she feels herself to be in. She needs now to find a way of defending herself from the wounding accusations now being hurled at her by all those affected by her allegation. Despite having endured the agonizing process of making an allegation of physical or sexual abuse, the abuser still dominates the child's world. It may be that for this particular child, the accused adult has been found guilty by the court. If this is the case, then the child will be made aware that he is about to serve a prison sentence. As a result of her allegation, all or some of her brothers and sisters may have to go into care, and the child herself may be poised to embark upon a very uncertain journey into the care system. Before the wheels of the system had begun to turn, the child may have fantasized about the relief she would feel, having managed to escape from an intolerable situation that occurred in her home. The reality may prove to be completely different.

Earlier fantasies of revenge on the perpetrator must pale into insignificance compared to the anxieties and doubts which now beset the child. Perhaps the family is split in their opinions and verdicts. Some may feel pity for the child and anger towards the perpetrator. But there is just as much chance that there will also be waves of anger and denial from those in the child's family who feel there has been a miscarriage of justice. The child may not be believed or worse: there may be a pocket of thought that the child has maliciously invented the whole story and is either a liar or intrinsically bad. There exists, too, the very delicate matter that has become public knowledge that mother and daughter or father and son have been rivals for the sexual favours of the adults involved, which is likely to arouse very primitive feelings and emotions.

It is likely that at some point in the unfolding of the trauma and the taking to task of the offender, the child will be overwhelmed with panic and fear. Perhaps she questions not only the wisdom of whistle blowing but also her integrity: 'Was I to blame? What did *I* do to make him want to touch me sexually? I wish I could put the lid back on it all – this is all much too frightening. Everything feels out of control. I used to lie in bed fearing what could happen — but this feeling of absolute aloneness is much, much worse.' Such are the thoughts that may crowd in on the child. In addition to her self-doubt or mounting confusion, it is likely that she will condemn herself and question whether the abuse really warranted all the fuss and interference, or could ever justify the dreadful drama of the courtroom. It is likely the child will question whether her need to put a stop to the abuse was worth disrupting the entire fabric of her family. For some children it may feel as if they have thrown a hand grenade into their own homes and everything is exploding, and now the terror is very real. Slowly it dawns on the child that although she is now physically removed from her traumatizing environment, the trauma itself is just as raw. In essence, she has not really escaped at all. Indeed she could experience the outcome of a 'successful' allegation as having stumbled into what Hunter (2001) calls 'the sinking mud of despair'.

In this highly charged emotional state, the child may well stare grimly over the edge and might experience a wave of longing to give in to the urge to go into emotional freefall. She may crave to feel nothing at all, to become numb or able to switch off all the noise and for her world to fall silent. She may feel that she is as vulnerable as an egg that may crack at any moment. She may experience thoughts and sensations that appear to make her feel she is about to break into small pieces. She may feel she is about to be annihilated. The concept of annihilation is expanded in Winnicott's list of what he called 'primitive agonies': 'going to pieces', 'falling for ever', having no relation to the body, having no orientation; and complete isolation because of there being no means of communication (Winnicott cited in Davis and Wallbridge (1991).

There are children whose abuse, physical and sexual, has been so severe, so brutal, that the chances of a return home or a placement with foster carers or adoptive parents are minimal, at least at the point when they come into care. Indeed, even if their family home had been stable in the sense that their parents stayed together, it may now have broken up because one or both of the child's parents may have gone to prison because of what happened to their child.

Abused children do not want to lose their parents. Children who disclose abuse rarely want their parents punished, or understand that their parents could be punished as a result. Where the parent is removed (or, in many cases, where the child is removed), the child can regret making an allegation. If the child is abused subsequently, she may keep the secret to herself for fear that this will occasion more loss. What these children want is for the abuse to stop. They may experience very complicated emotions. Sometimes both love and hate are felt towards those who have abused them. The child may also feel a sense of guilt: was it something she did which caused the abuse?

Chaotic living is a characteristic of most of these children's lives, and one of the extraordinary things that may have happened to them can be the number of people who have come and gone in their lives and the number of places they may have lived. They may well have come from families that move a lot, maybe caused by one or both parents having had different partners. They may have brothers and sisters and half- and stepbrothers and -sisters, some of whom they know, some of whom they are unaware of. They may be unsure of the nature of some relatives: someone they think is, say, a cousin could well be a half-sister.[5]

When children come into care the pattern of movement and confusion can be repeated; notoriously, they undergo multiple placements. Hunter (2001) explains one aspect of what it can be like for such children:

> Because children in public care often lead shattered, discontinuous lives, information about them becomes fragmented and lost. Their sense of themselves and their worth is harder to maintain if no one can even remember, for instance, that they lived with Nan in Southampton before she died. These children lack the sense that people know them, know about them in the ordinary continuous way that children in their own birth families take for granted. (p.26)

It is important for the therapist to know and remember this detail about the child's life in order to earn her trust.

Such a history is exacerbated very often by how the courts and criminal justice system affect them. For example, not only may a child have to stand in court and give evidence of the most traumatic kind against her father, but she will sometimes have waited as long as 18 months before being called upon to do so. A study by the NSPCC (Plotnikoff and Wolfson 2005) interviewed 50 child witnesses, aged 7 to 17, 32 of them in sex offence cases. They said that they felt intimidated in court and some said that appearing as a witness could be as traumatic as the original abuse. Just under half said that they had been accused of lying; and more than half said that they had been very upset, distressed or angry, a fifth of whom said that they had cried, felt sick or sweated.

A life like this induces a sense of loss and rejection, a feeling of being alone in the world, of having to rely on one's own resources because the resources of others – so generously offered at the time – are withdrawn when things become difficult. It is not the child who gives up the placement but (in the child's eyes) it is the adult who gives up the child. Even where a child has learned from past experience not to invest too much in a placement, breakdown only confirms and reinforces previous losses.

Loss underpins many of the lives of these children; it is rather like the loss caused by death. In some ways, children who suffer the terrible losses to which we refer here, react in the classic stages of those who are dying: denial and isolation; anger; bargaining; depression; and acceptance (Kübler-Ross 1970). However, while the stage of acceptance for a dying person is about allowing a 'good death', an acceptance that death is a part of life, not a violation of it, the child comes to acceptance of her loss in a more negative sense: she accepts that life has done what it has to her, and that the means of surviving that loss or dealing with it is to detach herself from others, not to expect good of people; to doubt their intentions, not to trust them. This can then be translated in many cases into anger, sadism and a need for revenge. The model of the world that the child has arrived at is one that makes perfect emotional – and even intellectual – sense in the light of what the world has done to her. Her world has been tipped upside-down, and she experiences her own perverse universe where love equals sex, hate equals love, sex and love both equal pain. She sees through a glass darkly.

As a result of these distortions, children can become aggressive, detached and withdrawn, highly unpredictable in their behaviour, and programmed for failure. They can throw temper tantrums, kick, spit and bite. They are frequently self-destructive to the point where they can be suicidal. They may abscond, trash their homes, or steal. They may destroy the very things that are important to them. Their psychosexual development has been grossly distorted so that their behaviour towards staff, foster carers, other children, and even complete strangers, can be highly eroticized.

They are unable to trust people, because it is safer not to do so. They have lost a sense of who they are. They can be driven by an abject terror of having to face the fact that no one wants them. They are, in their own eyes, thrown-away children – 'poppies in the rubbish heap' (Bray 1997). This may mean that they take control of their lives by ensuring that others cannot get close to them; they can act to ensure that there is no reason why they should be wanted.

A child's perception of abuse will depend on many things. Older children may remember and know exactly what happened to them sexually, but for very small children, of maybe two years of age or even younger, their memory may only be experienced as a primitive terror. They will not have understood the sexual act, but they will have understood the horror of what it was like to be squashed and nearly suffocated. For them it is not about being sexually abused (though they were), it is about 'Did I nearly die?' But for children just slightly older the language at their command may be inadequate to describe what has happened to them. How can, say, a nine-year-old boy explain a sexual response to his mother's abuse or an eight-year-old girl how her father forced her to have anal intercourse? Their inability to find the right words goes hand in hand with guilt and shame. In these circumstances, the therapist helps the child to make sense of what has happened; for example, by working non-verbally through play, so that she may distinguish between parental love and a sexual act.

Being told not to tell, to keep the 'secret', as if it were some kind of pact between child and abuser, is also likely to increase the sense of shame; it may even make some children think that they may have been, at least in part, to blame because keeping a secret implies collusion. Also, some children will often be led by their abuser to consider themselves to be partners, rather than victims; and they may come to believe this. If a child gains advantage from the abuser because of the abuse by, say, gaining status within her family or being given money, this, too, can fuel a sense of blame.

Abused children may develop a profound sense of their own badness, they may feel that they have deserved what happened to them; this is something that will impinge on their sense of their own worth. Brier (1992) speaks of the 'series of quasi-logical inferences, characterised by the child's dichotomous thinking and egocentricity' which, he says, appears to proceed in this way:

1.   I am being hurt emotionally or physically by a parent or other trusted adult.

2.   Based on how I think about the world thus far, this injury can only be due to one of two things: either I am bad or my parent is (the abuse dichotomy).

3.   I have been taught by other adults, either at home or in school, that parents are always right and always do things for your own good (any other alternative would be frightening). When they occasionally hurt you, it is for your own good, because you have been bad. This is called punishment.

4.   Therefore, it must be my fault that I am being hurt, just as my parent says. This must be punishment. I must deserve this.

5.   Therefore, I am as bad as whatever is done to me (the punishment must fit the crime – anything else suggests parental badness, which I have rejected. I am bad because I have been hurt. I have been hurt because I am bad).

6.   I am hurt quite often and/or quite deeply, therefore I must be very bad.

Brier goes on to say:

The extent of self-hatred that these dynamics can engender is often startling as is its endurance. The power of the abuse dichotomy for the adolescent or adult survivor lies in its self-perpetuating qualities thus: 'I was (and continue to be) hurt because of my badness and the evidence of my badness is that I have been (and continue to be) hurt.' (pp.27–28)

Unsurprisingly, these children have lost their anchor in life and, with it, their sense of orientation and their ability to navigate the world confidently.

Exercises

1.   Imagine yourself in the following situations:

     a)   You are five years old and trying to keep up with some older children who have climbed a steep river bank, but are getting left behind. You begin to panic and your body starts to freeze still. Eventually, you feel unable to move and cling to the side of the river bank. If you don't move, you will lose any chance of catching up with your friends. If you try to move, your fear is that you will slip and fall.

          • What feelings does this scenario arouse in you?

          • How would you have coped with the experience?

          • What resources would you have had access to that could have helped you survive the experience?

     b)   You are an unborn foetues in the womb, floating, but attached by an umbilical cord to your mother. After birth, the cord is severed, but, after this seperatiomn occurs, your mother then enfolds you in her arms and offers you her breast. Now consider how you would feel is she dropped you. Imagine repeatedly feeling that you are not being held securely enough.

- How would you view the world if no-one came to attend your needs when you felt cold or hungry and simply left you alone?

- How would you view the world if the response you received to your cries to be held was a shout to be quiet?

- How would you view your place in the world if you experienced complete isolation because you had no means of communication?

2. Take a large sheet of paper. Draw something that expresses how one of the above scenarios made you feel. You could use clay or sand and glue to represent your feelings.

CHAPTER 3

Trauma

The structure of the brain

The brain is an organ about which the more we know, the more we come to realize how much more there is to know. Evolution and culture have affected the development of the brain, and we are being made aware about many other factors that affect its growth. For example, there is now a developing understanding of the importance of food and nutrients (Richardson and Montgomery 2005), so much so that science now suggests that Wodehouse's Jeeves was right all along: fish is good for the brain. Behaviour can be affected by what we eat.

The brain is an immensely complex piece of machinery: it has over 100 billion brain cells or neurons, including glial and ganglia cells, and each neuron has, on average, 10,000 synapses or connections to other neurons. We may be linked, through evolution, with other creatures, but even the most advanced chimpanzee cannot carry out the tasks performed by an average two-year-old. (Cohen 2002).

However, the brain is much, much more than a highly developed and efficient computer, able to carry out all manner of tasks and be the source of imagination and inventiveness that drives human progress. When we are babies we learn to become social animals. We come to understand the environment and other people around us, and we learn how they relate to us, how we act towards them and they then react towards us.

Very obviously, we learn much of this through the persons closest to us, usually our parents and, especially, our mothers. Loving responsiveness to a baby's needs helps to build neural pathways in its brain. These translate how the baby understands the way in which loving and healthy relationships work. The opposite is also the case: where a baby finds hostility and a lack of responsiveness to its needs, so its brain takes on different expectations. Thus, the brain is also the place where our reactions to the world about us are built.

Our brains develop most dramatically in the womb and in the first year of life as Cohen (2002) explains:

> The brain starts to be identifiable when the foetus is three weeks old as a slab of cells in the upper part of the embryo.
>
> In the womb, the brain develops far more than other parts of the body. As a result, when babies are born, their heads are very large in relation to the rest of their bodies. Two-thirds of the brain is present at birth. In its structure and anatomy, the newborn baby's brain is remarkably like that of an adult.
>
> At birth, the baby will have all its 100 billion neural cells in the brain. More brain cells do not sprout after the baby is born and becomes able to see, move and speak. Missing at birth, however, are most of the connections between the cells.
>
> As the baby feels, moves and perceives, these connections are created. From the outset, heredity and environment interact. The baby's individual experiences create particular pathways and connections between particular cells. A baby brought up in a dark room does not form the pathways for normal vision, for example.
> (pp.14–15)

As the brain develops, the foetus also becomes aware of its environment and is responsive to stimuli at about two months. Unless a foetus is sensorily impaired, it is able to taste, touch, smell, hear and see; thus, when a baby is born all its senses are intact. We also now know that both the brain and the body of a foetus can be damaged: drinking, smoking, drug taking (even prescribed drugs) can cause injury. Likewise, prenatal malnutrition can have its effect; and while even a mother's tension can affect a baby, traumatic stress that she may experience when pregnant (which could include rape or domestic violence) can have a seriously deleterious effect on her baby. A baby's brain can also be affected by deprivation before birth. Any of these influences can damage the growth of brain cells, and injury to a baby during birth can have the same effect.

The baby brain does not emerge fully formed at birth. As Cairns (2002) puts it, 'once the baby is born, the real work of brain building begins'. Babies are wholly reliant for their growth, indeed their very survival, on others, most commonly their parents. Soft words, gentle music, being held lovingly and talked to in a similar fashion, the warmth of the closeness of the caregiver's body – all these can be critical in the healthy development of children. But the reverse also holds: the baby who is not held, who is shouted at, who is surrounded by noise and sudden movements, is pushed, shoved or slapped, becomes an anxious, stressful and fearful child. Just as a foetus *in utero* can pick up its mother's moods, so a baby is even more sensitive to the moods of its caregivers.

In order for an infant to be able to think about feelings and be able to regulate emotion, there must be neural pathways from the higher brain to the lower brain. These are affected by interpersonal interactions. If the infant's primary caregiver has been unable to offer the kind of soothing and containing interactions that can create these neural pathways, some of this work may be done in the relationship with the therapist. But as YoungMinds (2004) explains:

> Research strongly suggests that the quality and content of the baby's relationship with his or her parents may affect the development of the neurobiological structure of the infant brain in a way that is harder to alter the longer the relationship patterns endure… Whilst we need to understand much more in this field, we are learning about serious, long-term consequences of neglect, trauma and abuse on early brain development and subsequent physical, emotional and social growth. (pp.1–2)[6]

Cairns (2002) explains the relationship between attachment and the growth of the brain:

> Attachment behaviours are the key to this early infant brain development. Stress is toxic to the brain, causing profound changes in the brain structure and function in the interests of survival. When

the baby attempts to engage the caregiver through attachment behaviour, the urgent desire is for the caregiver to enable the baby to modulate and recover from the stress which has provoked the behaviour. Babies with available and responsive caregivers enter into a relationship in which each attunes to the other and together they experience relief of stress. Both baby and caregiver will go through a cycle of stress arousal, stress modulation and the pleasurable experience which follows the soothing of stress. Most babies (55–70 per cent) are fortunate enough to have such a relationship with their caregiver. (p.49)

Where such positive caregiving takes place, 124 million connections at 24 weeks gestation can be found on brain tissue the size of a pinhead (Karr-Morse and Wiley 1997). At birth this is 253 million and by eight months the number could be 572 million connections. Thus, by eight months of age, the baby's brain has produced the maximum capacity for versatility and flexibility and this number of connections are more than is needed.

Cairns (2002) goes on to explain the 'very different picture' when caregiving is inadequate to the task of the baby's optimum development:

On the one hand the lack of interactive stimulation leads to a lack of production of some brain connections and a 'pruning' of connections already over produced and not being used. There is thus a qualitative difference between the brains of securely and insecurely attached children. Securely attached children develop bigger brains.

On the other hand, the failure to modulate stress arousal leads to the nature and location of those connections which are made being different. Confronted with persistent unresolved stress, the infant brain forms characteristic use-dependent structures, of either hyper-arousal or defensive dissociation: hyper-aroused infants show perpetual signs of distress and irritability, while dissociated infants show none despite being in a physiological state of high arousal. (p.50)

The effects of trauma on the brain

The implications for children who are abused are all too obvious. A child does not have to be beaten about the head for brain functioning to be affected. The pathways that Cohen (2002) describes can be affected by other forms of physical abuse, by neglect and sexual abuse.

Discussion of how trauma affects the brain, or of the effects on the brain of, say, food, raises age-old questions about nature and nurture. It used to be the case that biological and psychoanalytical explanations were seen as inimical to one another. Indeed, one recent writer has gone so far as to state that 'for the first time a full biological explanation of our social behaviour is becoming available' (Gerhardt 2004). She goes on to refer to 'unseen patterns that are woven into our body and brain in babyhood', which, as another writer has remarked in response, 'is an attempt to break away from the dichotomy of nature versus nurture' (Caviston 2004).

However, most people would not regard either approach as cancelling out the other. There is an element of truth (given how much we still do *not* know about our makeup) in both explanations. Biological science has taken enormous strides in the last 50 years, or even less, and the neurobiologist and the psychoanalyst now have much to learn from each other and much to agree on. What we are and how we have been brought up are far more closely related than any exclusivist view will allow.

Ziegler's (2002) definition of trauma is useful: 'Anything that disrupts the optimal development of a child can be defined as a type of trauma to the system.' Trauma can occur before birth – a mother can herself be physically abused which can affect her unborn child, while her smoking, drinking alcohol and taking drugs can also affect the child. Poor care in pregnancy and the mother's own emotional instability can also have negative effects on the baby.

After birth other negative factors can have their impact: separation from the mother, her lack of interest in her child, lack of stimulation, and so on. However, for our purposes and for those involved in child protection and the care of abused children, trauma is associated with physical and sexual abuse and neglect.

Ziegler (2002) reports what he calls 'the most serious finding' of the past decade – that neglect has the most long-lasting effect on development and is the 'most persistent and pervasive' form of trauma. He goes on:

> The concern is not only how the brain reacts to neglect as a threat to survival, but also what the brain is *not* doing while preoccupied in survival mode. Neglect shifts the focus of the infant away from the exploration and essential learning the brain is prepared to do at the beginning of life. (p.37)

However, we should be careful about believing that a traumatic event has a predictable outcome. What we can say is that *some* kinds of traumas affect *some* children in *different* ways and that this will depend on the type of trauma, the age of the child and the circumstances she was in at the time it happened. James (1994) explains:

> Psychological trauma occurs when an actual or perceived threat of a danger overwhelms a person's usual coping ability. Many situations that are generally highly stressful to children might not be traumatising to a particular child; some are able to cope and, even if the situation is repeated or chronic, are not developmentally challenged. The diagnosis of traumatisation should be based on the context and meaning of the child's experience, not just on the event alone. What may appear to be a relatively benign experience from an adult perspective – such as a child getting 'lost' for several hours during a family outing – can be traumatising to a youngster. Conversely, a child held hostage with her family at gunpoint might not comprehend the danger and feel relatively safe. (pp.10–11)

James's use of the word 'overwhelms' is a very necessary one. Trauma, in its clinical sense, is more than its popular connotation with shock. The experiences that come as a result of trauma are so overwhelming as to be, at times, uncontrollable. Thus, one can feel, literally, helpless, vulnerable to the point of a fear for one's self, experience a loss of safety so that one feels wary of others, and loss of control so that one's actions become unpredictable. This is the very opposite of what healthy development requires, when we need to be assured of our contacts with the world and others. This is denied the traumatized child, the child who, as we said earlier, is thus propelled into emotional freefall.

Children react differently from adults to trauma. Thus, trauma can affect a child's sense of identity, development, trust in others, management of her behaviour, and so on. Some of these may be present in a traumatized adult: for example, a woman who is raped may well be affected in her ability to trust others. But, for a child, trauma is very likely to be much more far-reaching and more likely to affect seriously general social and individual functioning.

Children will often regress when traumatized. They revert to a state of helplessness. They can (like adults) adopt adaptive responses so that, for example, they avoid intimacy, feel that they need to be in control, and act in ways that deter relationships and closeness with others. They can experience flashbacks, hyperactivity and dissociation. These, in turn, can affect their education and lead them to be diagnosed with various behavioural disorders. Depending on their age, they may turn to drugs and alcohol abuse and engage in promiscuous sexual relationships.

The four major effects of trauma on children are a persistent state of fear, disordered memory, avoiding intimacy, and 'dysregulation of affect' (James 1994). This latter effect is when emotions seem out of control: the person feels about to burst with emotion and may be overwhelmed or overwhelm others with it if allowed to do so. For children, this can show itself in play by fantasy, movement, speaking almost in voices, together with uncontrolled emotional outbursts unrelated to the play. Children can also exhibit this 'dysregulation of affect' by being defiant, anxious, uncooperative, depressed, impulse-ridden, acting unpredictably and being oppositional (James 1994).

Another result of trauma is dissociation, which is when painful and traumatic events can be presented with an absence of emotion or appropriate emotion. This can be misinterpreted. Something that happened many years ago may be able to be talked about dispassionately (but, of course, that may not be so). Something that has been discussed many times may lose its edge. But, as Hunter (2001) explains, dissociation is 'an internal psychological state which we assume is present when a usual or expected involvement emotion is absent' (p.98).

Another serious consequence of trauma is its effect on attachment, and this we deal with in the next chapter.

Ziegler (2002) explains one reaction to trauma as follows:

> For traumatised individuals, emotions have lost their usefulness in providing important information to the reasoning centres of the neocortex, and emotions become a runaway train that catapults the child into the past and face-to-face with previous traumatic experiences. It is not effective to say to a traumatised child: 'Calm down, you are overreacting.' You might as well say this to a passenger on a plane that is coming for an emergency landing. Who are you to decide what is overreacting? (p.150)

Common responses to trauma are fleeing and freezing. In an attempt to flee the situations, traumatized children may cry and alert caregivers to provide protection. Tantrums and aggressive behaviours may be part of this strategy. But as children are mostly unable to flee, they commonly resort to dissociation, although some children do abscond. When they feel threatened, children may, instead, freeze in order to take in the situation and work out what to do. The adult response to this can be to threaten and demand, which then increases the child's fear.

Freezing is usually seen as the child being oppositional-defiant. This is a conduct disorder when negative, defiant, disobedient or hostile behaviour is shown towards authority figures. Common signs and symptoms are temper tantrums, arguing with adults, actively defying rules, deliberately annoying people, unfairly blaming others for mistakes or misbehaviour, being touchy or easily annoyed, angry, resentful, spiteful or vindictive. All this can mean that the child can suffer socially and academically.

The trauma bond

Trauma can be deceptive. A trauma bond may have the semblance of a secure attachment within a family. But the trauma bond and secure attachment differ in that attachment is based on love and the trauma bond is based on fear and distorts the child's perceptions. She lives in a state of underlying uncertainty, dependency and apprehension, and so seeks to appease the abuser, to meet, even anticipate, his needs and demands. Children affected by the trauma bond exhibit behaviour that is geared to meeting the needs of the adult or what the child perceives those needs are. This in itself can create a blueprint for future relationships, suggesting that they are best conducted by being servile and dependent. The child as she grows can develop a victim mentality, can become attracted to, and invite relationships with, powerful people who cause harm and help to reinforce the blueprint. For adults, the trauma bond can influence how they see themselves as parents.

The classic case of such a bond, albeit from a very different area, is that of the publishing heiress Patty Hearst. A group calling itself the Symbionese Liberation Army kidnapped her and she ended up as one of 'them', taking part, apparently uncoerced, in bank robberies. This identification with her captors became so extreme that it was symbolized in her being renamed Tania.[7]

More recently, Gregory (2004) has written of her childhood as a victim of her mother's Munchausen syndrome by proxy, whereby, at times, the child began to feel that if she was constantly being taken from hospital to hospital to hospital, having health check after health check and treatment after treatment, she must, by definition, be ill and thus receive treatment.

Ziegler (2002) says of the trauma bond:

> It may seem strange to say that survival can be promoted in negative ways, bur this idea is the reality for many abused children. These children develop negative bonds that promote their survival, which are called loyalty bonds or trauma bonds. If someone holds your life in their hands, they are very relevant and powerful to you. Pleasing such a person, or at least not displeasing them, becomes critical.

Such an experience can rapidly change an individual in lasting ways. The rape victim, the prisoner of war, the hostage, and the abused child all have similar experiences.

Many children do not have a frame of reference to be able to call trauma an unusual experience. Many of these children do not have a good sense that the trauma is over, even when the situation has ended. Therefore children tend to continue the loyalty and the trauma-bonding response to a life-threatening situation, long after the events are past.

Exercises

1. Find out as much as possible about your early life: find old photographs or home videos of yourself with your parents or siblings. Did you take family holidays? If so, where did you go? Think about the happy times and the frustrating or angry times. If you have your own children, can you see any similar patterns in their lives?

2. Imagine yourself at other ages. Were there any traumas in your life? On a sheet of paper, list your recollections of any traumatic experiences and rank them by intensity.

3. Consider recent traumatic events, including wars, terrorist attacks and natural disasters, that have received a lot of media coverage. Do you think that media coverage of the events and other people's reactions and fears have affected your own responses to these events? If so, in what way?

CHAPTER 4

Attachment, Separation and Loss

John Bowlby was a key figure in developing attachment theory in the 1950s (see Bowlby 1969). This theory states the idea that a nurturing and positive relationship in our earliest months, or even before birth, allows us to make satisfactory relationships as we go through life and to develop maturely. Bowlby (1979) wrote:

> Attachment behaviour is any form of behaviour that results in a person attaining or maintaining proximity to some other preferred and differentiated individual... While especially evident during early childhood, attachment behaviour is held to characterise human beings from the cradle to the grave. (p.129)

However, should that early experience be one of violence, rejection, pain, abuse, lack of bonding and disruption, then our maturing will be stunted and we will have developmental problems. At worst, these can show in criminal, violent or abusive sexual behaviour. Children who have suffered long periods of separation from their parents or who have lost their parents and suffered severe emotional difficulties find it extremely difficult to make relationships with others and can become withdrawn. They can exhibit various other kinds of behaviour problems. While the ability to make attachments is formed in very early childhood, its effects can feed through into adulthood so that it affects adults' personal and sexual relationships and their ability to parent. Howe (2000) writes that 'attachment behaviour is an instinctive biological drive that propels infants into protective proximity with their main carers whenever they experience anxiety, fear or distress'.

Originally, the child–parent relationship was emphasized as the formative one by attachment theory. It obviously remains critical but we now know that other relationships can be influential on our development and affect our ability to attach.

The internal working model

Archer (2003) refers to internal working models as 'road maps' and Burnell and Archer (2003) say that the model:

> maps out the most suitable response-routes to familiar, and unfamiliar, challenges. [These models] reflect the child's view of, and confidence in, the attachment figures' capacity to provide a safe and caring environment. Moreover, these models, in turn, organise the child's thoughts, memories and feelings regarding attachment figures. Inevitably, they will also act as guides and predictors of future behaviour for the child and analogous attachment figures, such as adoptive parents. (p.65)

The internal working model (Bowlby 1969) is the cognitive representation of early attachment relationships. Based on attachments with primary caregivers (e.g. secure, avoidant, ambivalent, disorganized), children develop beliefs and expectations about themselves, others and life in general. Levy and Orlans (1998) explain these as: 'I am good/bad, lovable/unlovable, competent/helpless'; 'caregivers are responsive/ unresponsive, trustworthy/untrustworthy, caring/hurtful'; and 'the world is safe/unsafe; life is worth living/not worth living'.

These early attachment experiences become internalized as core beliefs and anticipatory images that influence later perceptions, emotions and reactions to others (Levy and Orlans 1998). Internal working models are not entirely conscious but, once established, are resistant to change.

However, with appropriate experiences the child's internal working model can change and become modified.

Howe (2000) explains how the internal working model can be based on one of the following types of attachment:

- secure (the carer is loving and the child is loved)

- ambivalent (the caregiver is inconsistent in how he responds and the child sees herself as dependent and poorly valued)

- avoidant (the caregiver is seen as consistently rejecting and the child is insecure but compulsively self-reliant)

- disorganized (caregivers are seen as frightening or frightened and the child is helpless, or angry and controlling).

YoungMinds (2004) explained how mental health problems can result from early negative experiences:

> The vulnerability of babies and toddlers to mental health problems is increasingly acknowledged. The effect of these problems on subsequent functioning – physical, cognitive and emotional – is being investigated widely. Research strongly suggests that the way in which the brain develops is linked to early infant relationships, most often with the primary carer. Whilst other relationships in later life can be crucial, for example relationships with adoptive parents, these primary infant/carer relationships have a key impact on the mentally healthy development of the child...
>
> Active, satisfying and reciprocal relationships with parents create a basis for a sense of inner confidence and effectiveness. (p.1)

Children who have been abused often suffer from a lack of attachment due to harsh, even brutal, experiences in infancy and childhood. They are affected deeply by loss. A child who has been abused can still feel a sense of loss of the person who was the abuser.

The formation of our sense of self, of our identity, is complicated and delicate. Critical to it is our ability to form mature, loving and trusting relationships with others. Our ability to do that is shaped very much in our earliest years. This attachment is what is lacking for those whose experience of trauma, loss and abuse ruptures the process. Therapy seeks to restore it.

Touch

Touch is one of the most fundamental and powerful ways of establishing relationships. It is central to the formation of early attachment relationships and involves loving and caring touch, with sensitivity and an awareness of boundaries. Children with attachment disorder, who have been sexually and physically abused, can become very defensive when touched and afraid of physical intimacy. In working with children who have been deprived of appropriate physical nurture and who have been inappropriately touched, this is an important area for consideration.

We recognize the power and importance of touch, but a potential professional dilemma arises when thinking about touching between a child or adolescent and her therapist. Unless the child's key carer is involved in the therapy – which is not the norm but does occur if therapist and manager think it helpful for the child – the therapist is alone in the therapy room with the child. Clearly, there are opportunities for positive touch if initiated by the child in her play. However, in so vulnerable a setting a therapist cannot engage in touching activities such as hand or foot massage, however potentially therapeutic these might be. There is always the danger that activities between therapist and child which are meant to soothe and nurture could be misinterpreted by the child and turned into something quite different from the therapist's intent. The child can become sexualized or can panic because she experiences a flashback that involved her being groomed for an adult's sexual gratification.

When playing or moving together during therapy, touching may occur naturally and spontaneously; obviously the therapist would not pull away from the child's touch. Horne (1999) says:

> An experience of the body as potent, to be enjoyed...is important
> for the developing baby, as is the mother or carer's capacity to meet,
> understand and enjoy the communication involved. Where the

communication is one of distress, the infant needs the mother to make sense of this and respond in a way that both alleviates the distress and does not leave the baby with an overwhelming feeling of uncontainment 'falling to pieces'.

...a colleague who observed Sikh friends with a new baby boy noted that part of his care involved his mother oiling his body and lovingly massaging his limbs and torso – an interaction clearly delighting both. While this example may be culture-specific, the need for the baby to feel that his body, and therefore his person, are wanted, understood and valued is an important one. The quality of touch in containing and confirming body boundaries can be seen in this vignette, as can the mother as active participant with her infant, calling forth and 'meeting' his capacities and ventures. (p.32)

However, children who have been abused often replace this kind of benign and comforting touch with something which is aggressive and invasive. Perplexing acting out of children pushing away adults – often aggressively, sometimes violently – can commonly occur both in residential homes as well as during therapy. Without knowing how behaviours are linked with previous memories and experiences, the carers and therapist may be shocked and confused. Physical injury inflicted by a child on an adult needs careful processing after the event. Supervision needs to be made available as soon as possible, and support given to the carer or therapist. Without provision of this emotional holding, the event can threaten to overwhelm both the adult and the child. Children will need to know that the adult has survived their attack and, more importantly, that he understands the attack was more than something personal. While children will continue to be made to understand that adults will not submit to blows and will restrain the child in any outbreak of violence, there can be discussions aimed at helping the child to find that she can put things right and at helping her and the adult to try to identify what was going on in her mind before or during the outburst.

Maltreated children and children with attachment disorders 'have an inordinate need for punitive and/or coercive control of others', say Levy and Orlans (1998), which effectively means they feel incapable of developing a positive rapport with carers or their therapy working alliance. The authors continue:

> These children are extremely emotionally defensive. Although they experience sadness, worthlessness, rejection and fear, they generally only allow the direct expression of anger. They feel empowered by demonstrations of anger and aggression.
>
> They learn at an early age that anger works: if others retreat in response to their anger, they believe they have won; if others escalate in response to their provocation, they also believe they have won, because they have engaged others 'on their terms'. Certain caregiver or therapist responses, such as anger, helplessness or emotional distance, serve to empower the child's negative patterns... (pp.116–117)

The corrective attachment therapy, say Levy and Orlans (1998) is based on the idea that the development of a:

> new belief system – internal working model – is a primary goal of treatment. Children with attachment disorder operate with negative core beliefs: 'I am worthless, defective, unlovable; carers are unsafe, unavailable to meet my needs; I must control others to survive'. (p.117)

What they go on to describe as a 'negative working model' has its roots in, and develops as a consequence of, pathological parent–child experiences, such as abuse, neglect and abandonment. The provision of safety and containment should send curative messages to the child or adolescent. The message is that the therapist will survive such attacks and continue to provide a caring relationship, in spite of what has just occurred. These are what Levy and Orlans call 'chronic power struggles' and 'control battles'. These are tackled by a thorough understanding of the child's modus operandi.

When considering approach or techniques with children as damaged as Lucy (see the case example on the following page), it is interesting to see how the interaction between child and therapist fits with what Winnicott has to say about the importance of following the child. According to Kahr (2002), Winnicott felt it was particularly important for the therapist not to lead, for it was the child's 'initiative, creativity and aliveness that he regarded as most precious and which he hoped would be able to release them from whatever it was that threatened to impair or to imprison it. Anathema to Winnicott was anything that might lead to compliance, to that existential death from which he most particularly hoped to be able to free those with whom he had dealings' (p.*xxv*).

Lucy: *The swaddled child*

Lucy, a 14-year-old, had become very involved in one therapy session in role-playing a parent (a father, her therapist felt). The therapist acted the young child who was trying to make up her mind which imaginary sweets she wanted to 'buy'. The 'child' was unsure and hesitated, which seemed to trigger a sudden and unwarranted outburst of anger, and Lucy/the father figure kicked the therapist sharply at the base of the spine, aiming, the therapist assumed, at his posterior.

Boundaries within therapy demanded that the role play should end, and Lucy was told firmly that physically hurting another was not permitted. Her reaction was extremely defensive: she stood with her hands on her hips, legs firmly planted and leant down on the therapist, her face a livid red. She shouted loudly: 'How dare you?!' and threatened to lock herself in a cupboard in the therapy room, where she announced she would harm herself. She shut the cupboard door between them, and the tension increased as both struggled to contain the sudden heightened arousal. Swift intervention was required.

Calling through the door, the therapist told Lucy that he felt that she had wanted him to experience bodily how it had felt to Lucy to be subjected to a sudden and aggressive attack, one that she had not deserved. While Lucy had needed to make the therapist feel how dreadful this felt, she had lost control and now (said the therapist) she felt that the therapist might punish her in some way, either by retaliating physically or withholding affection.

Lucy was assured that the therapist had survived her attack and wanted to show her that he understood where the need to strike out had its origins – namely her early memories and sensations of being hurt by an adult whose role was to protect her from unwanted attacks because she was a small child. After several minutes of reassuring her that she would not be rejected or hurt, Lucy slowly emerged from the small room. A large stretch cloth was gathered up and Lucy was offered one end, with the suggestion that she tie this firmly around her waist and that the therapist would do the same with the other end of the fabric. With visible relief, Lucy did so, and eye contact was made from the distance that separated the two of them: Lucy expectant and clearly distressed, and the therapist not a little affected by her acting out. It felt strongly that they were now connected to each other both physically and symbolically, significantly as if by an umbilical cord in the space that existed between the anxious, angry child and the therapist.

The therapist told Lucy that she could wrap herself in the cloth, which she had rehearsed many times before. She grabbed hold of the fabric and moved around and around, until she travelled the few yards that separated her from the therapist. Within seconds, she was at the point where the therapist was standing, expectantly, with his arms outstretched. The large frame of an adolescent girl was instantly 'delivered' swaddled in the soft material, powerfully held and contained. At this point, the therapist felt that they could safely come together, and a much younger and trembling Lucy was firmly held and embraced.

Lucy was then told gently that she would be allowed to unravel herself when she felt ready, and also that the therapist would watch her play and explore how it felt to experience bodily being free to leave and return to an expectant 'other', over and over again.

This was repeated many times and on the last few 'returns' to what both accepted, albeit symbolically, was a secure base, Lucy actually showed how she experienced emotionally what had happened by saying 'Mummy, Mummy' quietly to herself.

Exercises

1. Describe your first day at primary school. How did you feel when you saw the person who took you to school walk away? How did you feel when you were collected from the school gates at the end at the end of the day?

2. Have you been in a relationship that was ended by the other person? Did you feel that you or the relationship had been abandoned and, if so, how did you come to terms with this? What effect did the experience have on your sense of 'self'? How did you 'move on' from this relationship?

CHAPTER 5

Therapy: Establishing the Framework

The most productive therapy is child-centred, which means that the child leads. The therapist's motivation is driven by the child's needs. For example, in cases where the child denies that a traumatic event has occurred, a therapist will stand by his own assessment of the child and avoid direct conflict or argument over the subject, working in a consensual way. The emphasis on child-centred therapy should not be taken as meaning the therapist is passive or colludes with avoidance and denial.

The role of the therapist

Who is the therapist?

A therapist has several concurrent roles, which include being:

- a witness to the child's story
- an advocate for the child in relation to other professionals
- someone who empathizes with the child and affirms the validity of her experiences.

He needs to be compassionate and emotionally warm, the kind of person to whom children are drawn, with whom they want to spend time, and who is able to enter into the child's experience and able to speak the language of the child.

Perhaps the most essential quality is for him to be able to contain the child's experience. The child must have confidence that the therapist will contain her intense feelings. It may help to tell the child that he has worked with other children who have been hurt by adults in a similar way.

He is trained to hear appalling stories and witness the acting out of painful experiences in the child's therapy sessions. He is critical to the child's recovery. Each child will be assigned a therapist based on an assessment of the child's needs. The therapist's relationship with the child can be a very significant one.

What the therapist must know before he meets the child

Therapy requires good preparation before the child and the therapist actually meet. The therapist must do everything he can, before he and the child get together, to attempt to understand the child and the experiences that she has undergone. This can be achieved by a thorough reading of the child's files and meeting with significant people who have been involved with her. The case history will be particularly important in determining significant people and their part in the child's history. This will be especially helpful at a later stage when the names of some of these people appear in symbolic play.

The perceptions of past carers and others may help the therapist to gain some understanding of the child's emotional development and why, for example, she acts in certain ways. This allows him to gauge his starting point and what to expect from the child. The therapist also needs to know and understand the child's culture. An understanding of a specific culture may also help the therapist to understand the child's thought processes.

It is also vitally important that there is close working between the therapist and the therapeutic parenting team. The child must be aware of this and feel that she is held by the alliance. This means that there has to be good communication between parenting team and therapist, and attention given to how the child is handed over at the beginning and end of each therapy session.

The therapist depends on communication from the care workers about what is significant or concerning in the child's life. Before a therapy session the therapist also needs information about medical matters (e.g. injuries, health concerns, illness, complaints of symptoms); significant occurrences (e.g. whether an incident, like violence, absconding, or self-harm has occurred); and what is important in the child's life (e.g. staff leaving, contact with family). This can be done by using detailed records, telephone, or what occurs in the waiting area between therapist and residential care worker before and after the session. The child can be included in this or not as appropriate. But where the child is present, she shouldn't be made to feel shame (about, for example, behaviour) and shouldn't be asked intrusive questions about therapy. In all of the above, it is naturally essential to keep records of any significant events.

Structure and boundaries

To ensure that the task of therapy is clear, consistent and safe, it is necessary to define the basic boundaries. This provides a benchmark from which all specific needs can then be assessed and evaluated. Before the therapy starts, the therapist and carer will explain the important boundaries within which the therapy will be set. Children should not only *be* safe but they should *feel* that they are safe. This means that they must have the assurance of the therapist by the provision of boundaries that nothing bad is going to happen to them; that they know what is happening and why; that the session lasts a specified period of time. It is important that children are contained emotionally and physically.

The frequency of the therapy sessions should be fixed and is normally a single, one-hour session a week. The therapy will normally start and end at the same time each week. Sticking to the times acts as both an actual and symbolic focusing for the child. Carers who bring the child to the sessions should be made aware that they are critical in the times being adhered to, and that even if the child gets to sessions on time each week she should not be brought in a rush.

The therapist should always be available on time and remain available for the duration of the session. The session should end an hour after the planned start time. If a child refuses to attend a therapy session, the key carer can work with this during the hour, either at the therapy room or at home. The therapist remains available in the therapy room throughout the child's therapy time.

It is important that the child understands the rules about what can and cannot take place during the sessions. The therapist should explain the basic rules, such as that neither the child nor therapist will be physically hurt during the session, and that the room and toys should not be damaged or broken. The therapist will also explain what will happen should the child try to hit or injure the therapist: the normal response would be to ask the child to stop, but if the therapist is unable to help the child to stop, assistance will be sought and the session may need to end. If necessary the therapist will get help to restrain the child physically. Inappropriate sexual behaviour towards the therapist will need to be managed carefully so that boundaries are clear without inhibiting appropriate communications or play. The importance of safety cannot be underestimated. It is what Bannister (2003) calls 'the key to successful therapy, even if that meant things moved at a slower pace'(p.14).

The therapy room

The therapy room, where the child and therapist work together, should be somewhere where the child wants to be, somewhere which is warm, comfortable, bright and child-centred. The room should be welcoming to the child, rather than overly clinical. This is the child's stage: a place where she can express herself and allow her imagination scope and freedom. Images on the wall should be ones that encourage the child to feel safe, that conjure up tranquillity, that have the effect of calming.

SACCS has therapy rooms and a reception area with brightly painted walls of rural scenes that look down on comfortable sofas, toys and books. The corridor to the therapy rooms is also painted with bright scenes of fields and trees, and the carpet and a path painted on the walls allows the idea of children walking along to a destination. Each room is individually themed. For example, one room is designed like a house, with painted fireplace, picture, videos and books, and looks out to a painted garden; another room has a seaside theme with the walls adorned with cliffs, sea and beach for water and sand play; and another, painted with clouds, is where children can be boisterous, with more than the usual number of toys (including a puppet theatre) and with curtains at one end which they can turn into a theatre to stage plays or enactments.

The therapy room is where a space is created in which a relationship is established between therapist and child. The child can act out her story, express herself freely and get in touch with her own feelings and emotions. The therapy should be, as Chethik (2000) says, 'conducive to the child's play, so that her internal life can unfold'. He says that it 'should be an open stage, where the child's imagination can be expressed without restraint in an atmosphere that allows her to reveal what she thinks and feels' (p.51).

At SACCS children's own art work is kept in small containers to which only they have access. Before children go into the therapy room they choose an adhesive picture, created to their personal preference, to put on the door of the room. This both marks it as their room while they are there and allows them to make that clear to others. Abused children have been so disempowered that even the smallest ways by which they can assert themselves and allow them some control over their lives should be encouraged.

All rooms have an alert button, so that the therapist or child can use it to summon the attention of the carer outside. ('Alert' is a far preferable word to 'panic' with the latter's dramatic undertones.) On hearing the alert button sound, or any other noise that causes concern (i.e. for the safety of child or therapist) the carer or therapy room supervisor should knock on the therapy room door, open the door and ask if any help is needed.

All materials and toys for the therapy are available in the therapy rooms. The materials should be chosen because they are useful in facilitating communication and have potential symbolic use. Their use is, however, as unlimited as the imagination of the child using them (Tomlinson 2004).

The therapy room should be equipped simply with items such as large beanbags, table, chairs, clock and mirror. Toys that should be available include toy animals, cars, human figures – male and female, black and white, enough to represent the child's family life and others – sand tray, string, telephones, puppets and dolls, crayons, painting materials, and a small shelter, such as a put-you-up tent.

Within the integrated model it is important to distinguish the task of therapy, with the emphasis on communication (play), rather than the kind of nurture that will be provided through therapeutic parenting that takes place in the home. It is not the task of therapy to meet a child's regressed needs through primary provision associated with feeding and other forms of physical nurture. Therefore, the materials provided in therapy will have a symbolic rather concrete quality (e.g. a toy baby feeding bottle rather than an actual feeding bottle).

Toys and other materials that the child brings to the sessions should not be taken into the therapy room unless this is agreed, in advance, by the therapist and residential worker. Toys and materials are available there.

Toys and their symbolic use

Play reveals meaning, even if that meaning is not immediately recognized by therapist or child. Toys become invested with significance. They can also be used to test children's reactions, as well as to encourage them to say what they may be slow to say. Toys are ways in which children can relay their experiences of sadness, anger, happiness, fear, trust, guilt, and other emotions. However, while the therapist may have his own ideas about the symbolism of the child's actions, it is the child's interpretation that is most relevant.

The use of toys also allows children to communicate less directly. They may not have the verbal skills, or even concepts, to speak about what happened; and given how painful their memories may be, they may not be able or wish to do so. This indirect communication through playing with toys, which can be as revealing and vivid as any words, can be less damaging to them.

When Madge Bray and Mary Walsh (see The Story of SACCS on p.141) built on special times and play, they developed their toy box technique, which has been used with great effect in helping abused and traumatized children to communicate. As Boyle (1991) describes it:

> ...the approach...is based on a willingness to receive, at the child's own pace, whatever it is that the child wishes to impart. The adult...listens, responds and sets the boundaries. Creating warmth and trust comes before making any attempt to impose her own adult agenda onto the process. Showing a willingness to enter into the child's own world and interact with them at this level is the overriding characteristic of her work. She sits on the floor with a toy box and creates an environment where play is the natural medium of communication. Using toys and the simplified language of the child, she is able to introduce us to this world, so that we glimpse close up the confused and contorted experience that is inflicted by adults oblivious to, or uncaring of, the consequences. (p.*xii*)

Toys can be used either as a trigger by the therapist or as a means of expression for the child. A therapist may choose to use toys like the following ones for these purposes:

- *Mr Punch* could represent the abuser (he does after all beat his own wife and child), or be representative of dark thoughts harboured by a child.

- *Woodpecker with three chicks in a nest.* This glove puppet is useful because the mother bird is detachable. The toy can be used to explore ideas of abandonment and neglect, as well as feelings about parents.

- *Lamb,* another glove puppet, can be shown to be sad with her bleating and ability to hold her head down, and can help externalize children's feelings of sadness.

- *Doll* with a fixed smile, pink cheeks and blue eyes, who appears to be saying that nothing worries her. But if her dress is opened (and clothes should only be removed with the child's permission), it reveals a heart. When this is opened, inside is a small, sad version of the large doll. Such dolls can be black or white, male or female.

- *Courtroom toy box* with the figures in a case – judge (or magistrates), lawyers, police, witnesses and accused – together with courtroom furniture (the witness box can be called the 'telling the truth' box). This can be used to prepare children for a court appearance.

- *Furry glove puppet* which, turned inside out, ceases to be cuddly and benevolent and becomes fierce looking, with one protruding teeth and claws. This can symbolize the way parents and other adults can change from appearing to be protective figures to those who threaten and abuse.

- *Telephones* allow children to speak to the therapist indirectly.

- *Clam shell* glove puppet is held tightly shut and the child is asked what is needed for it to open. This can help children to say what the therapist needs to do for them to 'open up' emotionally: make sure the clam is safe, that it is spoken to gently, and that it is shown that the therapist and child care about it.

- *Furry rabbit* that trembles in one's hand when the circuit is activated by the dampness of the holder's skin.

Children who have been abused are children who have been rendered powerless. The use of toys and their own imaginations allows them to speak creatively about painful experiences in a way that is palatable to them.

Bringing a child to therapy

Although therapy makes use of play and art materials and movement, the child may still feel threatened. Many times she may state that she can't paint or can't dance and may feel too tense to play. She may say 'I don't know *what* to play' and may need the therapist to support her to do so, by sitting with her. The therapist will reinforce that therapy is not about being good at anything. Everything in the therapy room is provided to meet the emotional and developmental needs of the child, and therapy is never judgemental. The key carer who brings the child can help ease her anxiety by supporting the philosophy. For effective therapy to occur, it is also crucial for carers to acknowledge that going to therapy will most likely be painful for the child, as she will have to confront memories and get in touch with experiences that she may have previously denied taking place. In order to offer effective support, the carer must be attuned to the child's current feelings.

Effective therapy can only take place if the child or young person is supported emotionally in her living environment. With this always held in mind, the role of the carer who brings a child to the therapy rooms is an important one. During the session it is important for the following reasons that he waits outside the therapy room in the reception area:

- If there is an accident or incident, having a familiar carer nearby is vital for proper support and action. It is essential to have a safe, secure environment.

- It is important that the child feels emotionally secure and knows the carer is waiting, and that if she feels unwell or needs the toilet, and so on, the carer is able to offer attention, help or nurture.

- Children do sometimes become overwhelmed in therapy and decide to leave early.

- The child needs to experience that the worker supports her therapy. This is done most obviously by being physically present and available throughout the therapy time.

- If the child sees a carer as unsupportive then her mixed feelings and resistance may become even more confused or difficult.

A child being brought to therapy is likely to have distorted ideas and anxieties about the way in which adults communicate with one another.

Therefore, to talk over the child's head or behind her back may be seen by her as secrecy.

Experiencing openness and being treated with respect by adults is likely in itself to be therapeutic and empowering for the child. This might mean allowing the child to be directly involved with the handover between carer and therapist. Of course, the degree to which the child can be involved in communication will vary according to her age, level of functioning and what the particular issue is. For example, while it may seem appropriate that a 15-year-old is present during all discussions about her therapy it might not be appropriate for a 6-year-old. This can be discussed, agreed upon and changed over time as the child develops and matures.

Chrissie: How the truth emerged from play

Chrissie was referred for longer-term therapeutic work and an assessment because the social worker thought that her behaviour indicated some sexual abuse, but so far the child had made no allegation or disclosure.

Although Chrissie was ten and felt she was far too old for toys, it was not long before she became involved in play. Through her chosen use of puppets it was not long before she started to play out her family history. She had one older brother and one younger sister. The three of them were placed in the care of the local authority, at three different foster homes. Chrissie's younger sister had no recollection of events at home when they lived as a family. The older brother made it clear that he had a high regard for his father and wished to emulate him when he was older. (As he grew older and went through therapy, his high regard turned to hatred.)

Chrissie was aware that her therapist also knew her brother and sister and was always keen to have information about them. In time the therapist realized how fearful Chrissie was about the possibility of him passing on things she had about a family secret. Eventually, through play and talking, what emerged was that the family secret – which had been solemnly maintained by the whole family – concerned the children's involvement in sexual abuse. As therapy progressed, Chrissie came to trust her therapist more and more, eventually telling him that her father had sexually abused her. She also said that she was entirely to blame.

All the literature indicated that the therapist should tell Chrissie that she wasn't to blame and that her father was totally responsible. This he did but she told him: 'How do you know, you weren't even there?' To tell a child that she is not to blame when she has a deep feeling of responsibility and guilt is not really helpful.

Chrissie was very young when the abuse had occurred ('I was in my nappy') and so the therapist decided that, as Chrissie enjoyed using puppets in her play, he would use them to help her to understand the role her father took. For weeks they played out a scenario with Chrissie, as a child, trying to stop the therapist, as an adult, getting her to do something and how difficult this would be, especially as she was no more than a baby.

They played out how the therapist (her father) would ask her to go to a certain place (she had been called to the bathroom where the abuse took place and she believed that she had gone willingly). She would say no, and the therapist would pick her up and carry her – after all she was still a baby. Eventually after many weeks, she turned to her therapist and said, 'Of course, I couldn't have stopped him. He was big and a man. I had no choice and it was entirely his fault.'

This was a revelation to her and a weight appeared to lift from her. She became very angry with her father and went on to deal with all the issues she needed to deal with in order to move on.

Exercises

1. Consider a child with whom you are currently working. How does she view:

    *   herself?

    *   her care providers?

    *   you?

    *   the world she lives in?

2. Write down ideas for how you could improve her sense of self-worth and her trust in you, her carers and the rest of the world.

3. On a large sheet of paper draw your ideal therapeutic environment. How might the child with whom you are working view your design? How does it relate to her needs and past experiences?

CHAPTER 6

The Search for Lost Boundaries: Therapy Tasks

According to Meekhams (1993) all creative acts, whether choreography, science or research, occur within a recognisable creative process. She points out that this creative process is commonly considered to be cyclical with four stages, quoting Hadamard (1954) and Poincare (1982) when defining the stage as:

- preparation
- incubation
- illumination
- evaluation.

These four stages offer useful guidelines for movement or play therapy, as all four occur within the relationship between therapist and child. In the preparation phase the therapist will explain the rules and boundaries for therapy (as discussed in Chapter 5) and make preliminary assessments of the child's play or movement. The child may be feeling apprehensive, perhaps wondering what they might uncover during therapy.

This stage involves building the child's trust in the therapist. This is not easily achieved given that those whom she should have been able to trust, such as her parents, may have abused, deserted or failed to protect her, while others, such as her carers, may have come and gone in her life.

Traumatized children will have learned that not trusting can be a means of self-protection: if you don't trust then you won't be disappointed, hurt or abandoned. Much emphasis should be placed on the child's perception of safety during the therapy sessions – indeed without this being established, any attempts to move forward will flounder, and could even be perceived as harmful.

The incubation stage provides what Winnicott (1971) called the 'potential space' or creative relationship between the therapist and the child. Play is an important part of this relationship. The therapist can now observe the child clearly immersed or 'incubating' in her creative process. The child can become engrossed in play, perhaps burying small figures in the sand tray, or repetitively playing out a scene that may – or may not – be significant. The important point during this stage is that it is not clear precisely what the symbolism is, or where it could lead the child and therapist. But the beginning of symbolisation marks a willingness on the part of the child to communicate personal and complex feelings and issues to the therapist. Meekhams suggests that at this stage the relationship between the therapist and child could be seen to 'mirror the merged state of mother and infant' (2002, p.17). Communication is often non-verbal as the child has not yet learned to express her needs by speaking about them.

At this stage intervention should be kept to a minimum, the space should be held, and the child be allowed to experience letting go and not knowing, but doing so in the presence of a benevolent adult. It is thus very important not to seek a false sense of knowing. Here the therapist needs to tolerate uncertainly, not knowing, even bewilderment, while helping the child to cling on to what they know and can control. This opens the possibilities for play and creativity.

The illumination stage is where meanings become apparent and the child may be encouraged to reappraise her experiences. A child's willingness to engage in symbolization signifies a willingness to communicate difficult, painful and confused things to the therapist, all of which make up the pattern of the child's own life and psyche. The urge is now to come to an understanding, to make sense of what is happening and has happened. This is accompanied by a shift in perspective, which can fundamentally alter the child's view of the world and herself. This can be exciting or sometimes distressing.

Evaluation is an active stage where the place and importance of therapy is more openly debated. The child can now absorb that what is played out in therapy is part of her healing process. She needs to be able to relate the insights or 'illuminations' that took place in therapy to her life outside the therapy room. Only at this stage can the child and her therapist begin to prepare for an eventual ending. This could involve a formal review of her therapy, looking back over the times and experiences shared together. Ending therapy is discussed in greater detail in Chapter 9.

Children who have been abused experience fear, anxiety, depression, anger and hostility, and they lack self-esteem. They may act in sexually inappropriate ways. Browne and Finkelhor (1986) say that such children have experienced 'invasion and erosion of physical, emotional and social boundaries'. Attempting to talk about what has happened to them can trigger in them high levels of anxiety or provoke overwhelming feelings of rage, and provoke them to physical or verbal aggression, which can then lead to dissociation. A child may have used this mechanism in the past as a way of surviving abuse, but when she engages it as a way of coping when no real threat any longer exists it can become dysfunctional. Dissociation can reduce the victim's ability to attach words to feelings, to symbolize or fantasize because, as Kelley (1984) remarks, no child has a vocabulary for what should have been 'an adult experience' because the abuse happened at a pre-verbal level of development. The perpetrator may have also threatened to harm the child if she spoke about the abuse.

Research has shown that the creative process, when the child is engaged in play, art, music and movement, can restore self-esteem (Franklin 1992; Stember 1980), allow for a reawakening of physical sensations, which are often blocked out following sexual abuse (Carozza and Hierstiener 1982), and can help suppressed feelings to be expressed (Sagar 1990). What Cody (1987) calls 'the search for lost boundaries' is facilitated by the therapist providing a wide range of materials for the child within the therapy room. Play, art or movement therapists provide the potential space for the child to use toys, toy animals and miniature vehicles, or to choose what they want within the therapy room. They can act out their non-verbal explorations of 'what is inside or outside the self' (Cody 1987).

Sagar (1990) has described how sexually abused children often choose to make messy mixtures which may be spread on any surface or are put into containers for the therapist to keep safely. Thus, the task of the therapist is to recognize that messy packages or configurations of any play medium can 'represent the secret which the child formerly had to keep', as Sagar puts it. If the child can be encouraged to engage in this form of playing out, it allows her and the therapist to work towards integration, in a 'concrete and sometimes ritualistic way'.

Some therapists see their giving permission to make a mess as particularly significant for sexually abused children. 'The mixing of paints, water and other liquids and materials, to be kept from week to week in containers was frequently described,' says Cody (quoted in Murphy 1998, p.13). 'Sometimes these were potions to kill or heal.'

A therapist may use a technique of acting as a container for the child's 'spilling over'; he may sit alongside the child as paint or a runny substance runs over the edge of the table, making sure he puts paper on the floor to catch the over-spill. This can be played out over and over – the child will experience an adult holding and containing symbolic ventilation, that is the child expresses her strong feelings safely through symbols.

If we look to the example of Kate (see the case example below) we can see the effectiveness of another form of communication: mirroring, which is based on Winnicott's observation that babies:

> use their eyes to convey their feelings and their needs; and they use their eyes to take in the feelings and communications from those around them. Eye contact is one of the core means by which we communicate and build relationships. Gaze avoidance or an inability to sustain eye contact is an important signal about the state of the relationship or the emotional state of the individual involved. (Kahr 2002, p.79)

Winnicott (1971) described how vital it is for the infant 'to see his mother's face reflecting and responding to his own state of mind, not frozen or preoccupied' (p.94). Therapists are attuned to his theory because it offers insight as to where a child may be functioning developmentally.

Kate's need for mirroring

Kate was ten when she came into SACCS' care. Her mother had lived with an alcoholic husband who subjected her to repeated physical assaults. Overwhelmed and defeated by her physical and emotional bombardments, Kate's mother had literally retreated from her role as mother. It was to her father, then, that Kate had been forced to turn, at an early and vulnerable age, in order to get her physical and emotional needs met.

From birth, Kate had grown up with domestic violence: shouting, screaming and horrifying fights were the norm between her parents. Kate's mother's finger was severed, and she was burnt or 'branded' on the legs. The impact of these frenzied attacks, which Kate may well have witnessed, will have left their own mark on her developing neural pathways.

Kate was holding on to her key carer with both arms, while sitting on the sofa in the reception area. Therapy was not a new concept for her, but when the therapist introduced himself Kate nestled into her carer, burying her face in his upper torso and neck, as some children do with their parents when overcome by the presence of a stranger. This is appropriate attachment behaviour for a young infant, but Kate was now 14, having been in SACCS' care for four years. She looked comfortable with her male carer; they seemed easy and natural, as he gently patted her arm, his head inclined towards her. There appeared to be a positive connection. With a reassuring smile and clear eye contact with her carer, Kate listened to him repeating that he would be waiting outside the therapy room if she needed him. At this point, Kate seemed to have regained a sense of emotional equilibrium and was then able to disentangle herself physically. As if emotionally buoyed up, she allowed herself to be calm and listen to what this particular stranger had to offer.

When the therapist began to speak to her, her breathing became shallow and audible, her face became flushed, and she was responding to explanations about playing and moving together in therapy with an enthusiasm that was immediate and spontaneous. Although, on one level, her physical impatience to get going was positive, her lack of 'stranger anxiety' and caution was also clearly visible. With barely a backward glance at her key carer, she broke away and rushed off to the therapy room she had chosen for her first encounter with the therapist.

From the first moments of therapy, Kate presented as being in a state of heightened excitement and was prone to explosive bursts of loud laughter, which were percussive and seemed, literally, to burst out of her, often incorporating whole body involvement, before recovery.

A warm-up began with Kate and the therapist sitting on chairs opposite each other, with a clearly mapped-out space between them, which they agreed neither would invade however enthusiastic or tempting it might be to do so. The therapist emphasized the importance of her firmly placing her feet on the floor and distributing her body mass evenly within the chair space, so that the base was solid. From this position, the focus was on deep breathing, with each placing their hands on their rib cages, feeling them expand as they filled with air, and exhaling using their voices to make sounds. The idea behind this simple exercise was to slow down Kate's breathing, and for her to try to get in contact with her body in order to start work, helping her to modulate her feelings and emotions.

Kate found this virtually impossible to sustain, bursting into lusty laughter. It seemed she had to laugh off or cut off from any sensations that might lead to getting in touch with her centre or body core, which would evoke emotions. While in this controlled proximity, the therapist would initiate an activity that focused on motivating Kate to join in with some gentle movements. Maintaining eye contact, the two would mirror a simple sequence of hand movements that occurred in the space between them, but were primarily shapes that Kate introduced. Thus, Kate moved, and the therapist mirrored these back to her.

Kate became animated when she imitated the therapist and when she was herself imitated. They clapped hands, made very loud animal noises and experimented with sounds their bodies could make when patted or beaten, Tarzan style. It was as if they were establishing mother–baby games that normally originate within the first year. Enactment such as this allowed the discharge of feelings in a creative way and equally afforded the opportunity for the therapist to match the intensity of Kate's emotions as they took turns roaring at each other.

Why venting the emotions must end in a sense of order

We have seen how children are allowed to give voice to their feelings and are given permission to make a mess in their therapy session. The licence to do this comes within clear boundaries. Although a child can do so with sand, water, clay, a combination of art materials, toys and dolls, any outpouring of emotions has to be restored to a sense of order by the end of the session. This may seem to create limits, but the psychological reasoning behind it is not restrictive. The therapist needs to guide a child who has little (if any) sense of time by being mindful of the approaching end to a therapy session. Drawing attention to the fact that the child has only ten minutes left before the end of the session serves to help the child begin to ground herself in the present and to help her understand that she is working within a creative process that needs to stop soon. As the session nears its end, the therapist will begin to restore order, inviting the child to watch or become part of the process. She may choose simply to watch the adult clearing and ordering, which in itself is a positive experience and one that the child may never have experienced in her early childhood. In addition, the therapist is mindful that the child may have invested meaning through non-verbal clues, hidden within her creative 'mess'. She may need the therapist to identify or pick up her communication, even if she denies this later.

The therapist can gain valuable insights into the child's inner world and turmoil by skilfully asking a child *what* she is wiping off the walls or floor or ceiling. It may be that the child responds by laughing or even leaving the therapy room abruptly, without explanation. It may be that this gentle entreaty is enough to provoke the child to respond in a way that allows true insights. It may transpire that the sand splattered up the wall is symbolic of smeared excrement, or represents blood or bodily fluids. The therapist has to be acutely sensitive to the potential symbolic representation of the child's 'product', and be dedicated to remaining alert to the subtlest clues the child may be attempting to bring to the surface. The therapist should also be mindful that a child's therapy process continues for the full hour of the session, and that emotions will be raw and even unbearable. This way of working promotes the idea that restoration of a sense of calm and order is necessary for the child to regain a sense of the here and now. If, on the other hand, the child were to leave her session with mess all around her and no sign of order, or with evidence of massive outpourings without containment and acknowledgement of what had taken place, she may feel out of control and frightened. As Tomlinson (2004) reminds us: 'The ending is important and potentially difficult as it is about completing an experi-ence. The child's previous experience of endings may have been that he is abruptly dropped or cut off, with the result of experiences being incomplete' (p.90).

Importance is laid on giving the child time to prepare for the ending of her playing out, which gives her the option of completing her com-munication and time to think about the ending. Tomlinson discusses how difficult it could be for the child if she had a sense that she was being asked to tidy away what she had been doing, especially if the communication has been difficult. He says that 'it could also feel like being forced to make reparation for it' (p.90). The crucial factor is the element of choice being available, so that it gives the child other options and choices, while the therapist takes the responsibility for receiving and containing the child's communication by clearing away in a sensitive fashion. According to Ziegler (2002): 'It is important to give the child the ability to express what he feels and thinks without moralising or modifying the raw expression of inner pain' (p.151).

The therapy room is a place to allow the child to let out rage and anger so long as no one is hurt and there is no significant damage. We would concur with leading researchers in trauma work that expressive therapies such as play, art, movement, music, puppets, role plays, metaphor and narrative assist the healing process.

Task of the therapy relationship

As we have said earlier, the crucial role of therapy is to provide the 'potential space' for every child to explore her past experiences gradually, within the safety and containment of metaphor, so that she can play out her trauma in the supportive presence of the therapist. He works in the space between the child's subjective inner world and the objective reality of the external world, as unconscious images emerge within their symbolic playing out, and he seeks to discover how the child has defended herself in order to survive each of the emotional, physical and sexual assaults as they impacted on her body and developing brain.

The delicate restoration of a sense of balance in the turbulent thought processes of abused children can be aided in non-verbal ways; for example, playing out what has been done to them by using a toy car, a puppet or any other toy. This means that the safe disposal of the victim's abusive feelings is crucial for promoting long-term recovery from trauma.

Children and young people need to be supported emotionally in their living environment if therapy is to be effective. However, despite this it is highly likely that an abused child will feel that the therapist could be potentially threatening or untrustworthy, and so may feel impelled to act out her abusive feelings with the therapist. He will need to take charge and reinforce safety boundaries if the child becomes overly destructive and aggressive. What is imperative for developing a positive relationship is for the child to feel that the therapist is able to hold boundaries and be firm, without being judgemental or rejecting.

As Bannister (2003) describes, there are many challenges that will emerge as the therapy process unfolds:

> Our skills were difficult to measure. It was clear that abused children responded to us but it was less clear if, and how, children benefited from our work. Those who cared for the children often stated that 'difficult' child behaviours had reduced, that communications between themselves and their children was improved and that the children looked forward to the therapy sessions. The children themselves were usually eager to attend sessions, although painful and angry feelings were sometimes released... sometimes their behaviour appeared to regress and carers found it difficult to cope with ten-year-olds who wanted to be cuddled and rocked after they had got in touch with their own vulnerability in a session. (p.11)

The therapist is physically involved with the child's play even by playing alongside her. He is watching and reflecting and matching the intensity of the child's feelings evoked by her playing out and mirroring her movements. The therapist helps the child understand what has happened to her so that she may face her fear, externalize it, and put the past in perspective. Recovery should mean that what has happened to the child will no longer exert power over her – it will not shape her thinking, her actions, or her reactions to others or to herself.

Children who have been traumatized often lack self-esteem and have a very distorted sense of self. A sense of self tells us who we are and where we are. Therapy can be a means of developing and restoring the sense of well-being and identity. For this to happen a number of tasks have to be carried out. These are:

- helping the child to develop insights into her unique strengths, rather than focusing on her weaknesses and any negative sense of herself

- helping her to understand what has happened to her, where she is now and where she is going

- careful interpretation by the therapist of what the child is expressing through play

- challenging the child's distorted perceptions about herself and past events

- helping the child to externalize her inner feelings within safe boundaries

- apportioning blame and responsibility correctly

- exploring attachment patterns, both with the child's primary caregiver (usually her mother but sometimes her father), as well as her present carers

- helping the child to explore, through symbolic acting out, and recover her memories and feelings about past traumatic experiences that she may have avoided or suppressed

- identifying the splitting elements in the child's personality

- providing a safe and holding environment

- helping the child express her anger within safe boundaries.

Being allowed to express anger within safe boundaries means that the child is then able to acknowledge the love that she may still feel for the mother or father who may have abused her. She may feel an ambivalence toward them and others in her life to which she wishes to give expression and may need, too, to have the opportunity to mourn the physical and emotional loss of a parent who may have been sent to prison, and to have the opportunity, too, to express anger at the non-protecting parent; the therapist also offers support to the child when she mourns the loss of the good parts of her parents and does not judge or condemn them. At the same time, he reinforces with the child that parents have a duty to protect their child, and that adults do not seduce or have sex with children.

It is worth remembering at this point that, as Tomlinson (2004, p.49) says, a child's sense of identity 'grows through the opportunity that he has for:

- general interaction in the care setting
- considering her own and others' experiences and opinions
- receiving feedback about himself from others
- making positive contributions to others
- being acknowledged and thought about by others
- making choices and negotiating with others
- working through what he has experienced.'

Once the child has a sense that both the therapist and the therapy environment are able emotionally to contain her creative outpourings without shock or negative reaction, she will need to explore her complex feelings about the relationships within her family, which are often disrupted following allegations. The child will need to explore her grief and anger with an adult who understands the dynamics provoked by allegations and accusations and to be helped with her crippling feelings of ambivalence towards both the abuser and the abuse itself. If this can be done through using creative processes which embrace the child's urge to express feelings about important people through play, she will be able to give shape and form to anxieties and terrors that are buried deep within her.

Shame and guilt

It is common for a child to question, or be fearful of, her own role in the abuse, and to believe that she was in some way to blame for what happened. The degree of emotional damage is so intense for some children that no amount of trying to convince them otherwise is sufficient to alter their distorted perceptions. As Hunter (2001) explains:

Children think very concretely. If someone gives them 'presents' they feel that person must be kind. If someone lets them share alcohol or drugs, they feel privileged. The powerful can command even the language in which an event is described and thereby distort it. 'My Uncle loves me and gives me lots of presents' or 'I'm Daddy's special girl' can be words that distort and misrepresent the events they purport to describe... These children's scenarios of seduction are not happy and enjoyable. They invariably contain blows, hurts, pinches, aggression, threats. Words are often at variance with actions. No wonder such children watch me and my words so intently and refuse to be impressed by my linguistic skills. They fight for control of the session: they think that power is abused by adults. When they are in charge they are despotic, delinquent. (p.95)

The situation is even worse for a child who, physically or sensually, actually gained pleasure from the abuse. If the perpetrator was skilled at grooming the child, and no violence or force was involved, the child may feel an emotional dilemma: did she actually invite or encourage the behaviour?

The child may also often see that others think that she is disgusting and shameful, that she did something that led to her being raped or treated as she was. Hunter (2001) explains how the therapist–child relationship can parallel the relationship between a mother and her young infant, as she affirms that her child is lovable despite the dirty nappies. In the same way, the therapist can allay the child's fears that she is disgusting and reassure her that she is lovable.

The urge to vomit can become a need, literally, to spit out, if the child has been forced to engage in specific sexual acts. Through play with water or sand or using provocative art and play materials such as glue or thick paint, the child symbolically spew out toxic memories.

Therapy engages the child, and can provide alternative methods of revealing her sense of internal damage through the safety and containment of metaphor or through the use of fictional stories. Working indirectly by playing out a story, child and therapist can create new fables or rework known fables, in an attempt to find another solution, or alter the final ending. Sometimes it might be important to allow this painful final ending without attempting to 'make it better' or sanitize it by suggesting a more comfortable resolution. It may be necessary that children immerse themselves in the horrors that sometimes threatened their sleep or ignited their imagination to anxieties of unspeakable terrors, such as being eaten up, tricked and deceived by an adult whom they thought they could trust. *Little Red Riding Hood* shows how children's imaginations can work in this way. There is a sense that this way the child can think aloud in the supportive presence of the therapist, mirroring the ideal emotional setting of mother and child reading a potentially frightening story together.

If the child fails to find a safe, protective parent to 'keep her in a child's position', as Hunter calls it, without recourse to what Winnicott (1965) called that 'secure base' of a mother's concern, then the child 'could only flee internally from these traumas' (Hunter 2001).

Thomas: Lessons from the animal kingdom

Twelve-year-old Thomas maintained that 'animals and children do sex because they want to – it's their fault'. His therapist set out to find creative ways of exploring this strongly held belief and how to address his distorted sense of reality.

He had been removed from his birth parents along with his brothers and sisters and eventually placed for adoption with a sister. The children were subsequently removed because of physical abuse. He was returned into care and placed with SACCS. In therapy, both by talking and later by very explicit drawings, he slowly revealed that he had been extensively sexually abused in his adoptive home. He had been exposed to pornography and various sexual acts primarily by the female parent. He was missing her tremendously – he loved her – but he was able to say that he was also angry about the treatment he had received from her.

Thomas later revealed that he thought animals and children were to blame for sexual activity with adults. He was convinced of this – the therapist and child even argued about it. This distorted understanding enabled him to avoid the sense of being a helpless victim, making him a powerful participant – and this he liked.

His therapist wondered whether children, like animals, could be trained, tricked and rewarded to act in certain ways – like in a circus setting. They also explored together that children loved but also feared adults and felt driven to please and obey them. There may well be the additional complication of feeling pleasure and accepting rewards.

Gradually, Thomas accepted that the animals and children might not have been to blame. They, too, might have been victims, and such children, far from being punished for what had occurred in their early lives, should be loved and helped to unlearn the lessons of such distorted learning. Thomas was able finally to demonstrate silently through play with a boy baby doll, the victimization and isolation of the victim, and to accept the sorrow and empathy for such insults to his childhood.

Transference and counter-transference

Transference is the unconscious redirection of a person's feelings for one person to another person. Children may project feelings, attitudes and desires felt towards their parents, other family members or past carers onto the therapist. The therapist's emotional response to this transference is known as counter transference. The therapist needs to remain aware of whether he is accepting the child's attempts to push him into the role of a past figure in her life, and guard against inappropriate feelings on his part, such as resentment, anger or fear, as such responses may reinforce the child's earlier negative experiences.

Needless to say, the therapist's self-awareness, training and continuing use of supervision and consultancy are prerequisites for effective work in this area.

The reality of counter-transference, albeit in a different context to that which we are writing about, is given by Aiyegbusi (2004) who explains:

> As professionals, we come to the workplace with our own traumas, losses and vulnerabilities, sometimes processed but sometimes unprocessed. Time and again we find that nurses and health care assistants who engage with this population of women [in secure psychiatric services] finding themselves disturbed by their work, occasionally to the point of breakdown. It seems that existing defences are no longer effective. The interaction between patients' unprocessed traumatic experience and that experienced by members of staff can amount to a toxic combination. Physical and psychological sickness is then experienced within the staff group...
>
> Processing such toxic emotional material is extremely difficult, given the potency of experience and since the counter-transference includes humiliation, exposure, rage and loss, the risk is that instead of processing, professionals act out within the staff group so interactions occur in hurtful ways, including bullying, aggressive practical joking, gallows humour, gossiping, or backbiting. Another way of acting out includes launching envious attacks on colleagues who are getting something good like a course or clinical supervision. (pp.52–53)

Having to absorb the projections of such children is something that faces all staff but, equally, they have to return them to the child so that they are experienced as benign. Hunter (2001) refers to 'trauma fragments' being 'toxic and powerful' and a professional hazard:

> I say this because such experiences stay with you and sadden and burden the recipient as well as adding to one's understanding. I have learned therefore to be cautious and respectful of my [patients'] reluctance to tell or revisit emotionally traumatic events. These happenings are hard to bear even at second-hand. (p.161)

Sexualized and sexually aggressive behaviour

Sexual play and experimentation is a normal activity for children as they grow up, as they learn about their own bodies and feelings and those of others. An important question is: is the child showing healthy curiosity or is she trying to get close in a sexually inappropriate way? Fantasy can take over and take on a life of its own. There can be a testing of reality. For example, a child who mutilates a doll to express her feelings may need understanding within the therapy session, but also helped to appreciate that there is a difference between what can be played out within therapy and what is acceptable in the outside world. One boy started to cut parts off dolls, swinging them round and treating them violently. He had treated violently a small child left in his care, and when such behaviour is left untreated it is not difficult to see it manifested in rape and other forms of sexual, as well as non-sexual, violence in young adults and adults. Or a child may act in a sexual way towards the therapist and ask him to do things to her, but he will tell her that while that's what she says she wants him to do, it is not what he wants to do and it is not something that adults should do with children. The therapist will attempt to make sense of the child's communication through this behaviour, while ensuring that the relationship between the two of them is desexualized.

Bannister (2003) makes a clear statement about how the fine line between inner and outer reality needs careful management in this complex and challenging area of work:

> Some therapists, including creative therapists, have expressed doubts about allowing a child to express violent play because it may either re-traumatize the child or may allow him to feel justified in behaving violently in other, appropriate settings. Prior [1996] states that, in fact, the child may be re-traumatized if he is *not* allowed to convey the reality of his experience in the only way he knows how. I agree with him that the child should be allowed to do this, but should be contained in a safe way so that he is not allowed to harm himself or others, or damage equipment. (p.62)

Referring to extreme sexualized behaviour in therapy, Alvarez (1992) refers to a child who:

> may masturbate in front of the therapist because…they wish to push into someone else the shock and outrage they were not allowed to express, nor even to feel… Now there is greater understanding that the child may need the experience contained by someone else who can stand it better than he can. (p.155)

She goes on to stress that the experience may still feel overwhelming and difficult to process for weeks, perhaps even several months or years.

However, if the child continues during a therapy session with highly sexualized behaviour, then the therapist should stop the session. To do otherwise may make the session unsafe for the child. For example, see the case example of Lottie (below).

Lottie: A small person who tried to do the impossible

Lottie responded quickly and dramatically to any opportunity in her therapy for role play. She would always set the scene and invariably she would be the adult figure, while her therapist would be allocated the role of young child. As trust developed within their relationship, Lottie gradually developed the scenario, which became specific and graphic, clearly acting out events and situations that she either had experienced herself or had witnessed.

One of the scenes she repeated many times consisted of a scenario involving the therapist being given the role of a child in an imaginary bath, with Lottie taking the role of an adult with a deep, gruff voice – presumably male – who was increasingly insistent that the child should allow him to get into the bath with her. The child/therapist firmly stated that he would not be allowed to get in and she told him to put his clothes on again and to respect the child's right for privacy. The child/ therapist further told him that if he failed to comply, she would call out for an adult to help. When this message had been clearly delivered to Lottie, the therapist then directed a technique specifically to address defining one's personal space and protecting that space.

Having 'de-briefed', with Lottie stating, 'I am not a man, I am Lottie', and with the therapist re-establishing who he was, they stood facing each other, adopting a wide, firm stance. From that position, the therapist traced the space overhead, to both sides and behind, defining his own space verbally as well as physically. Lottie was invited to mirror the therapist.

Having established their personal spaces, they played a game whereby one would stand still, allowing the other to walk towards him or her. The rules were clear and stated that when the person being approached felt the other was too close, he or she would shout 'Stop!' and this request had to be honoured. It was fun and yet powerful – especially when both experimented with one turning their back on the other, and using his or her senses to anticipate when the other was too close and making him or her feel uncomfortable. This was a simple yet effective way of dealing indirectly with the importance of being able to experience *taking back control* when the other person in the game backed away.

When engaged in acting out familiar scenarios of adults offering inconsistent and unpredictable parenting, an element began to creep into the enactment that the therapist found disturbing and needed to confront. Lottie directed the action and the therapist complied. However, a pattern emerged whereby she managed – extremely skilfully – to get too close to the therapist, having cornered him against a wall under the guise of the unfolding role play. The sudden physical change in Lottie could be clearly felt as she tried to grab the therapist's wrists and pushed her hips into his. The rapid breathing could again be heard and the rush of blood to her face seen as she struggled to remain in role.

The therapist would always manage to break free, sustaining his role and imitating a small child feeling suffocated and confused and shouting at her to stop because she was crushing him, and that she was too close or that he couldn't breathe properly. Lottie persevered in repeatedly launching herself onto or into the therapist, who felt it was time to name what was occurring and how it made him feel to be on the receiving end of her advances. It was time, too, to take control and stop the eroticized behaviour, as well as point out that it didn't feel like a game, despite her insistence that it was. As if sensing something like this was about to happen, Lottie suddenly increased her insistence, and pushed the therapist against a wall and tried to kiss him.

Mindful of the crucial importance of not shaming her or appearing punitive, the therapist brought the session to an end, informing Lottie that they would never use therapy sessions for trying to do 'sexy' things because he was an adult and she was obviously a child, and that included rubbing their bodies together and kissing. She was also told that sometimes she would have sexy thoughts or feelings and that this was part of growing up. However, she couldn't rehearse on the therapist, who also pointed out the possible dangers of doing so with anyone outside the safety of the therapy room. They could react aggressively or think that she wanted them to have sex with her.

The therapist put forward the idea that Lottie might also want him really to feel what it had felt like for her when she was small; to feel what it was like to try to get away but to be unable to because she was no physical match for an adult; to feel how she might have felt utterly helpless and emotionally, as well as physically, crushed. By making use of the non-verbal and the intensely immediate model of embodiment, (or experiencing the emotions related to trauma in or on the body), the therapist was able to give Lottie the chance to work over and over a theme of sexual bullying and to be permissive with regard to this, as long as she stayed within the boundaries.

Physically engaging with the child is similar to the notion of 'getting alongside', which also implies that it is pointless trying only to talk a child through her dilemma, but that one has to do it and feel it with the child. During what sometimes feels like endless

> playing out of a disturbing theme, by virtue of staying with the feelings evoked by the playing, it can help the therapist tune into the child and feel the disturbance on a physical level – which is where the abuse originally occurred.

Children who have been abused can become addicted to sexual behaviour. They can also be trying to find out, through their own means, what happened to them and why. They can replicate the abuser's behaviour. They can develop a feeling that because of what they have done (muddled in their mind with what was done to them) they should be punished. Such a feeling is confirmation that they are bad.

Alvarez (1992) questions the notion that it maybe helpful for the abused child to remember her abuse. She argues:

> I would suggest that a thought becomes thinkable often by a very slow gradual process, a process that cannot be rushed. The implications for the question of how the abused child may be helped to come to terms with his abuse may be that the 'remembering' may involve a million tiny integrations taking place, each one under conditions where other aspects of the abuse, other integrations, can afford to be forgotten. The abuse may have to be explored one aspect at a time; for example, what does it feel like to be told to lie down and have to do something when you have no say in the matter? What does it feel like to be told to undress when you don't feel like it and have no say in the matter? What does it feel like to be able to issue those instructions to someone else? How do they take it? All this may be explored via a doll's experience and, in many instances, that is exactly where it should be allowed to remain. (p.153)

While we should ensure that we do not collude with the denial of trauma, we need to be thoughtful of our attitude towards it.

Play therapy

Play is the 'emotional language' of children. It is something in which all children engage and, as Chethik (2000) remarked, it is difficult to function as a child therapist without understanding 'the extraordinary role of *play* – not only in a child's life and in the process of child therapy, but also in development and functioning in adulthood as well' (p.48).

Plato and Aristotle saw play as being a way in which children rehearsed adult roles, but it was not until little more than a hundred years ago that systematic theories about play started to be developed. Two theories of play have come to dominate our understanding of play: the cognitive development theory of Piaget (1951) and the psychoanalytic theory of Freud, which Freud developed, like his general ideas, from his work with disturbed adults. Later theorists have included Erikson (1965) and Sutton-Smith and Herron (1971).

Two other writers suggested the need to update Freud: Shengold (1988) said that to Freud's work and love should be added the capacity to play, while Plaut (1979) said: 'From a psychological point of view, love, work and play are the three ideal types of action.'

Within the context of normal child emotional and social development, play provides a special source of pleasure in dealing with naturally occurring daily living difficulties and the inevitable 'traumas' that impact on children, such as being left out of a game or laughed at or being the one left without a partner and sitting alone. It also provides an opportunity for children to make immediate connections with one another by playing together and offers a form of escape and fantasy, which can be a source of comfort.

Chethik (2000) sums up the value and function of play, as well as what it can mean for the essence of us as human beings:

> Through play the child develops and retains her fantasy world, her capacity and her imagination, and she learns to move comfortably between her inner life and her current reality. Gradually, this capacity to play and create is modified and, at times, lost as we become adults and as secondary process thinking and the reality process hold play. Adults who retain the capacity to be playful tend

to maintain an inner and outer world harmony. People who are humorous and have a capacity for playful metaphor are typically attractive to others. The creative artist usually retains a unique ability to explore his or her life and imagination and renders the images encountered to the world at large. The function of play is linked to the eventual capacity for fantasy, imagination and creativity, and the ability to play with ideas. (p.49)

For children who have been abused, and for other children in need of therapy, play therapy is a core therapy technique because play occupies what Chethik (2000) calls a 'special position between the inner and outer worlds it has many development-promoting capacities. The function of play allows a child to think about her actions' (p.49). For such children being helped to play may be important of itself because many with emotional problems have difficulty in being able to play, and this has the potential to affect their development.

Play therapy is a technique used to meet the child's need to experience on an emotional level how it feels to be able to expunge and jettison, or even punish, in a symbolic way through play in the safety of the therapy room. If the child or young person feels safe enough to be open and vulnerable enough, she can repeatedly go through the motions of trying to make sense of what has happened to her without having to talk directly to an adult. It is the task of the therapist, in this instance, to do what he is bidden and to hold the feelings of the child, by accepting the child's creations without judgements and advice. Interpretations are only made if the therapist feels it would be helpful for the child. If, however, the child is talking of taking her revenge outside the therapy room, the therapist will be firm in reminding her that there is a clear delineation between fantasy and reality and she will not be allowed to put this need for showing her rage into any physical reality.

A child or adolescent taking on a role of other people such as a 'father', 'mother', 'uncle', 'grandmother' or 'policeman' may, in the process, begin to experience what these others do, or think or feel. According to Chethik (2000), these experiences are important in the process of 'decentering'. Seen in the context of normal developmental usages, this process would help a young child move from her narcissistic self to empathise with others.

Winnicott (cited in Davis and Wallbridge 1991) noted that the capacity for play in childhood is linked to 'good enough' object development. Although a capacity for play has an innate component, it is clearly developed by the early parent–child relationship and dependent on the early playful object. Most 'good enough' parents naturally play with their children throughout the day.

Play, as we have said, is the emotional language of the child, and the therapist and the atmosphere of the therapy room should be conducive to the child's play so that her internal life can unfold. The therapy room should be a place where children feel comfortable to express their imagination freely and reveal their thoughts and feelings.

The child therapist must have the capacity to become a player with the child, to animate and vivify the unfolding material. This capacity forges a major link between the child and therapist, and enhances and develops the therapeutic alliance. Internally, the child links the therapist with the early pleasurable playful parent. The child also feels that she is in a special 'play space' (Winnicott 1968) with someone who can understand and speak her special language. As Oremland (1998) says:

> The original object – the parent – communicating effectively with the young child is there to enjoy the good, make right the bad, and render the ununderstandable understandable... Within the 'play space' the new object – the therapist – can help to make things comprehensible as the child plays out her internal world... Using the template of the parental object, the therapist can become the person with whom the most fear-laden areas of thought are expressed. (p.51)

The child's capacity to play has many diagnostic implications:

- How well and freely does the child play?
- Can she play alone in the presence of another?
- Is she too inhibited?

- Can she play with more than one person at a time (oedipal stage)?
- Is the play frozen, repetitive or stereotyped?
- Can she stick to rules?
- Is the play impulsive, wild and out of control?
- Can her imaginative – pretending and playful – capabilities unfold? Because 'the capacity for imaginative play suggests a harmony between the internal and external life, this is often an important barometer for effective treatment' (Chethik 2000).

Ideally play should be a mixture of action and thought. We learn a great deal about a child by observing her play and can assess her progress by following the quality of her play during the course of treatment.

Key carers involved in therapeutic parenting need to understand the importance of play in their child's daily life, not only during the therapy hour. Understanding the child's parent's capacity for playfulness will tell us a great deal about the child's family life: how have difficulties such as drug or alcohol addiction, domestic violence, poverty and other forms of impoverishment impacted upon the parents' emotional capacity for playing with their infant or young child? What are the taboos and restraints within the family? Were there any opportunities for pleasurable interactions? As Meekums (2002) says, helping carers and children develop some areas for mutual play 'may significantly affect the course of treatment by enhancing parent/child ties'.

Children are imaginative creatures who can turn a shoebox into something exciting: a cave, a tunnel, a house – the creative possibilities are endless. We know from the observation of healthy children that play is an essential way for children to make some sense of the world, to express their fears and concerns, to 'say' something. It also allows them to grow emotionally, intellectually, socially and physically. It is one of the ways they can express fantasies, and how they deal with stress and strain; it gives them a safety valve, and allows them to come to terms with fear and anxiety. It is one way that children are able to make sense of things and the world around them and is how even healthy children confront what scares and worries them. This is all the more so for a child who has been traumatized.

Play therapy is now long established through the early work of the pioneers of child psychotherapy like Anna Freud and Melanie Klein. Theories about play differ within each psychotherapeutic tradition, but each one holds to the central idea that play transmits and communicates the child's unconscious experiences, thoughts and emotions; it allows the unconscious to make unexpected connections. Play therapy is defined as a dynamic approach between child and play therapist in which the child explores, at her own pace and direction, matters, past and present, conscious and unconscious, that affect her.

Working with children through play and the expressive arts involves physical experiences, feelings and ideas. It links physical, emotional and mental experiences. Play can gain access to these early experiences and make it possible for the child to think about them and make sense of them.

Josephine: The little girl who believed she had to keep moving

Josephine was seven years old and felt very sad about her life. She and her younger brothers and sisters had been grossly abused; they had lost their birth parents and had been adopted. Unfortunately, Josephine's behaviour, her sexualization towards children and what was described by her social worker as 'psychotic-like' symptoms led to her being rejected by the adoptive parents. Diagnosed with post-traumatic stress disorder, she was finally placed with SACCS. She felt the loss of her original and then her adoptive identities keenly, and also missed her younger siblings, with whom there was no contact. She called herself Josephine Nothing and, in her therapy sessions, wondered whether she would ever belong to a family and have a name.

Her favourite toy at one stage was a ping-pong ball. Despite some rough play, against the odds this fragile object continued to survive. Josephine used to bounce or move the ball all the time. Once, in therapy, she was asked what would happen if she stopped bouncing the ball, and she replied very seriously that the ball had to keep moving or 'it would die'. It seemed she was identified with the toy and by using the toy in this way, she was able to explore her own emotional dilemma – as she saw it.

Josephine was often preoccupied with death and wishing to die. She was sometimes angry and aggressive to others, wishing to kill them. In therapy the therapist and child followed the little ball's adventures and the therapist wondered if it was 'a bit like you' in some ways. Josephine tolerated the comparison and continued to test and nurture her toy. When she moved to a permanent home many years later, she took the rather battered ball with her. Somehow, they had both survived.

The safe expression of feelings

Therapy offers the opportunity for the safe expression of difficult feelings that the child may experience as dangerous. For example, a child may feel anger towards a mother figure who seems very dangerous, both in the outer world where the child may fear retaliation, and in the inner world where she may wish to keep safe the image of a 'good mother'.

Anger often masks more vulnerable feelings, which are even more difficult to acknowledge and express. These can be fear and terror; despair; feeling rejected and worthless; feelings of self-hatred and self-blame; and sexual feelings, particularly feelings of pleasure or arousal, which the child may feel ashamed of or not understand.

Through symbolic play and expressive art work, these feelings can be expressed safely. When we express our feelings we communicate. The therapist is there to witness the child's feelings. What may have been experienced as unspeakable or excluded from consciousness can be communicated, and the child no longer feels alone. She can feel understood, although she may not be able to express in words the feeling or experience.

The therapist may reach the point where the feelings can be named and the therapist can help the child to identify and sort out feelings cognitively. This process of sharing, acknowledging and naming feelings and experience can help reduce any guilt and shame that the child may feel. However, before this the therapist must be able to receive and contain the feelings.

Emotional containment

The therapist's role could be perceived to parallel that of the mother of a young baby. The baby cries and the mother may not understand what is causing the distress, but she tries to find out. By physically holding her baby and attuning to her needs, she shows the baby that what she is feeling can be managed and contained. The mother is, thus, easing the baby's distress and giving her the opportunity to learn about her feelings and what happens when she expresses them. Gradually the baby learns that distress can be experienced without destroying her; it can be managed. This process is referred to by Bion (1989) as 'maternal reverie'. As the child gets older, she learns to do this for herself. As healthy adults, we learn that we can find the same understanding and comfort in periods of distress when we reach for others.

What the therapist offers is a similar kind of emotional containment. The function of holding and reflecting on feelings is most important. Feelings need to be received and accepted within the context of a supportive relationship before they can change.

Winnicott (1971) writes of the importance of the mother surviving the baby's real or fantasized attacks on her and responding to them without retaliation, rejection or moralizing. When the therapist is consistent, warm, accepting, not rejecting or judgemental, this is a very important, affirming experience for the child.

Treatment implies an active, involving process. But whereas medical treatment is often necessarily passive (that is, the treatment is done *to* the patient), therapy is active and the child is involved so that the treatment is done *with* her.

In Trevarthen's (2001) words, 'the mother sings, the baby dances'. This serves in some ways as a metaphor for what happens in therapy.

The use of body play in therapy

Young (1992) tells us that:

> the integrity of the body can be seen as central to the sense of self; when it is violated, the traumatic experience can become 'embodied', presenting the sexual abuse survivor with the problem of continuing to live in both a body and a world that is dangerous, damaged, or dead.

Sexual abuse is a bodily experience and its impact will be felt physically, emotionally and psychologically. The intention of movement therapy is to boost or repair the child's image of her body and her self by allowing her to express what she is feeling. It is *not* just about dance, but about all kinds of movement that the child chooses or is encouraged to make. Play is a natural activity for children and so is movement. Children move naturally to express their feelings and delight in the sensation of their bodies and movement.

But movement therapy is not only about the child moving her own body but also about what she learns, expresses and 'says' as she does so. It is also about how she perceives the movement or shape of other things. For example, in making use of therapeutic props and tools, we might use Lycra. Being a very flexible material, it can be dropped or moved about so that it forms shapes. The child can be asked what she thinks the shape is, which allows free association by use of words and in other ways.

Using movement in therapy has three main aims, which are to:

- help young people to reconnect the psychological and physical aspects of emotional experience

- interact in a group process to raise the level of how the child relates to others

- creatively gain access to unconscious feelings within individuals and the group.

This approach is concerned with the creative aspects of the unconscious, the symbolic expression of emotions through movement and imagery, which arise in the child's unconscious. A therapist's awareness of emotions, sensations, fantasies and images, and of how they integrate into the child's unconscious, is probably the most integral therapeutic type of benefit of movement therapy.

Meekums (2002), discussing dance movement therapy, explains that one of the key tasks of the dance movement therapist is to hold and contain the client's experience metaphorically, echoing but not precisely replicating a mother's holding and containment of her infant's experience. She goes on:

> The mother–infant relationship is mediated through eye contact, rhythm, sound, reciprocity, synchrony and sensory-motor experiences including holding... The mother responds through mirroring, modifying or elaborating the child's movements and sounds. She also crucially knows when to be quiet and cease to stimulate... The rhythmic engagement and disengagement experienced in a healthy mother–infant relationship and framed by the mother's attention to her infant's needs becomes a blueprint for the later ability to work and relax, to relate and to be alone. (p.33)

Abused children's responses to their bodies will have been so distorted that they will have lacked the rhythmic engagement and disengagement experienced in a healthy parent-and-child relationship. This can become a blueprint for the child's later ability to work and relax, relate and be alone. It is this positive blueprint which has to be re-made for the abused child.

Establishing a sense of 'body integrity' is a treatment goal for most traumatized children. Body integrity is a sense of wholeness and the ability to experience physical power, pride and mastery. James (1989) offers an effective description of this when she says:

> It is specifically indicated when the traumatic events led to the young victims feeling physically vulnerable, ugly, powerless, having no control over what is done to their bodies or believing their bodies are toxic – that is their bodies can cause fear, lust or loss of control in adults. (p.87)

It is of huge significance that trauma is experienced in the body, hence treatment needs to provide corrective experiences that impact on the child physically and psychologically. Van der Kolk and Greenberg (1987) reviewed studies conducted to determine how people organize their experiences, noting that some victims of trauma may lack the right words and, even, ideas to place the trauma in its historical context. They proposed that in this situation, a verbal approach alone – essentially, talking about it – may not be effective or helpful to the child.

According to James (1989), movement, music, body-awareness exercises and self-calming techniques (such as teaching the child to breathe deeply, visualization exercises) can provide the most effective therapy for children who have 'distorted body concepts'.

Exercises

1. Imagine yourself as a small child, playing.

    - Did you seek out play mates or did you prefer to play alone?

    - Did you enjoy imaginary play, perhaps with dolls or action figures?

    - Did you prefer playing with toys or being outdoors in a garden or park?

2. Did you have a special soft toy or object that was particularly important to you?

    • If you did how did it feel and what did it smell like?

    • What did you feel if you ever lose the object or felt that you needed it at a time when it wasn't available?

    • At what age did you feel you no longer needed it?

    • Where is it now?

3. Try to recall your earliest memory of your mother's and father's faces. Close your eyes and try to remember their smile, smell and tone of voice. Remember the hugs and kisses they gave you. Did they each express affection in the same way?

    • How did they respond if you were ill or hurt?

    • How well did they listen to you talk about your day at school?

    • Did they notice when you were anxious, even if you tried to hide it?

4. With another person, sit on the floor and face each other. Allocate a leader who will slowly trace shapes in the air, while the other mirrors the shapes exactly. Reverse roles. Discuss how it felt to be tuned into each other non-verbally.

CHAPTER 7

Themes in Therapy

A child who has experienced trauma very early in life, often presents in therapy with 'fixed, abiding difficulties in relationships' and with 'marked hyperactivity' (Hunter 2001, p.156). Hunter made reference to research by Perry *et al.* (1995) on brainstem development, which hypothesized that because the brain is developing neural pathways in early infancy, those pathways connected with the trauma are laid down early on and act as a basis for future development. This means that such children are over-sensitive to anything connected with the trauma and can develop into highly aroused children. Hunter goes on to ask herself: 'Could their restlessness be more correctly thought of as hyper-vigilance? They are constantly fearful, constantly defensive, constantly on full alert. It is these attributes that make them so difficult to tolerate. They are exhausting to be with' (p.156).

She uses the terms 'hyper-vigilant', 'over-sensitive', 'alarmed' and 'over-alarmed', which seem to offer helpful as well as accurate descriptions of children such as Marcus (see p.103). Whereas another young person or child would display only a mild anxiety on meeting with a new person, for Marcus and others about whom Hunter writes, simply being alone with a strange woman seemed to have been enough to spark off very powerful emotions.

Again, we turn to Hunter (2001) who tells of a young woman with whom she worked:

Children who have encountered hostile and abusive adults may need a therapist to be extra communicative and receptive, as the quietness of a therapy room may overwhelm the child who dreads being persecuted. This is no more than ordinary attunement of therapist to client, but it relies heavily on a therapist's awareness of experiences on the edge of being unbearable. For example, a young woman began her therapy with me by suddenly leaving the therapy room after 15 minutes, returning five minutes later and leaving before the end of the offered time. Several sessions of a similar kind followed this tentative start. Despite a 'cover story' where she would seem to take offence at something I said, it was eventually clear to me that she felt impelled to leave the room to keep our engagement under her own control and to avoid her feelings of claustrophobia. She told me much later that often she had been locked in the bedroom with her abuser. Interpretation of her fear for me had to wait until she could master it enough to take in my words. Initially her need in the room was to avoid my putting anything at all into her. Simple patient reassurance may be a necessary prelude to conversations that reveal feelings or fears. Therapists may need to hold onto what they feel for a longer time before they can offer it back as insight. (p.172)

A therapist working with a young person who reacts to situation in this way needs to heed the insight from Hunter, a therapist with many years of experience in this complex field, and to be ever mindful of the myriad possible interpretations. The child or adolescent will react or respond in a way that could set the therapist off-balance, and he must remain grounded and wait until sure of the image or memory that is driving the child to speak or act in they way that she does. It may be that the child is dissociating from any relationship that might threaten to bring further trauma. Therapists working with this level of disturbance can reflect on research such as that by Perry *et al.* (1995) who recommend as treatment 'anything that can decrease the intensity and duration of the acute reaction or disassociation' (p.156).

According to Cant (2002), therapy can be a forum for 'attacks on the boundaries'. Themes such as trickery and trust seem to be paramount. Often children new to therapy seem uncertain and unsure about how to fill the time they have in the session. Children can be, as Cant says,

> obsessed by what other children did in their therapy sessions, making many attempts to trick the therapist into letting the smallest piece of information slip…setting 'traps' in the room for the next child, or leaving hidden messages…these sort of skirmishes on the boundaries…were common and often designed to spoil something for someone else. (p.274)

Cant also refers to children attacking the possibility of receiving anything good.

Marcus: A lost childhood

What we know about Marcus's history is patchy, but such a fragmented biography is quite typical of many of the children with whom this book is concerned. Marcus came into care when he was nine. His mother was drug dependent and his father unknown. He had been severely physically abused by his stepfather, who, he claimed when interviewed by the police, had also sexually abused him.

He was repeatedly left in charge of younger stepbrothers and -sisters and was often left to cope with them at night as well. When Marcus was about seven years old he was discovered by the police hanging out of an upstairs window with his two-year-old stepbrother in the early hours of the morning and was taken into police custody. It was as if he had been driven to the point when he had to threaten his own life before he could finally alert the child protection services to his plight; in effect, he was demanding that they intervene on his behalf.

As an infant and young child he had several admissions to hospital with burns, scalds and bruising. Once in custody he again took responsibility for his own safety by requesting that he be adopted rather than return home. The manner in which he managed to escape from his intolerable living conditions served to highlight a failure of the system to protect him and his young brothers and sisters. However, his subsequent placement in foster care ended abruptly when his foster carer's grand-child accused Marcus of touching him sexually. His leaving was sudden, and there is little reliable information available clarifying conversations or explanations for his hasty departure. Three or four years after his foster placement ended, Marcus still speaks with affection about his foster carer and stalwartly refuses to acknowledge his having to leave as a rejection.

Marcus was brought to therapy for the first time by his key carer who waited outside the therapy room. He avidly avoided any eye contact with his therapist and moved swiftly and silently to a chair. The way in which he sat immediately caught the therapist's attention. His body seemed to be sinking through the chair giving a sense of wanting to disappear – to slip through the fabric – as his long torso folded over, his head and face completely withdrawn. It evoked an image of a hedgehog, sensing danger and retreating into its body for defence. As the therapist explained to him what movement therapy entailed and told him about boundaries of therapy, the therapist became more and more aware of the tension in the room. Marcus was not speaking, but his silence was extremely powerful. Although his body was held and taut in his hunched shape, his hands were clenching and unclenching with a steady rhythm. These repetitive movements in his hands seemed to be dis-charging an energy that was projecting not only fear but also what felt like an intense anger directed at the therapist. He realized that Marcus's reaction was extreme and the atmosphere was unsettling and he tried to address this by reflecting back to Marcus that the two of them would only be meeting briefly, but the therapist could hear the tension in his own voice!

Rather than continuing with the explanation of the therapy process until the end, it was decided that it was more important for Marcus to feel safe – he was clearly finding the whole encounter distressing – and the therapeutic task now was to respond to his hyper-aroused emotional state and provide him with an adult with whom he felt safe, in order to help him calm down.

When Marcus was told that he seemed to be finding being with the therapist distressing, and that his key carer would be asked to take him home, his relief was visible. When he returned to the adult whom he knew, Marcus almost instantaneously began to talk again and his body became vertical. He left with a hasty goodbye and no eye contact.

The therapist struggled to contain and make sense of what Marcus had forced him to absorb through his negative projections. His sudden and (what felt like) unprovoked anger had certainly stirred up some primitive fears. The therapist felt uneasy, but more than that – a feeling that he had done something bad, or at least was planning to do something to hurt Marcus. He had also had feelings of inadequacy and an overwhelming sense of having been rejected. It is possible that the situation in which Marcus suddenly found himself triggered an early memory that temporarily overwhelmed him and brought about a somatic and emotional reaction – and at the same time had little to do with reality. The therapist felt that he had not been given a chance to present himself as someone with whom he might be able to forge a working relationship and engage in recovery work. He had been dropped. Thus, we can see the truth of Hunter's (2001) remark, quoted earlier, that a young person like Marcus 'may need a therapist to be extra communicative and receptive, as the quietness of the therapy room may overwhelm the child who dreads being persecuted'. There is patently that need to do anything which can decrease the intensity and duration of the acute reaction and dissociation.

The image that remained with the therapist was of Marcus braced for some kind of encounter – fists clenched – but this was offset by another emerging image of a child in terror and on the verge of complete physical retreat into the body – cowed like an animal, knowing it was about to be overwhelmed and struck in some way. This child had clearly demonstrated – in the transference – that he was carrying, consciously or unconsciously, an intolerable burden and a rage that was talked about many times in the years that followed. Marcus later said that he feared its destructiveness and power and yet knew he had somehow to 'keep it under lock and key', because he thought he could kill.

What changed for him, over a period of time, was his awareness that his deeper rage could be directed at his stepfather who had physically, emotionally and (as was finally proven) sexually abused him as a young child. As Cant (2002) says: 'What these children have inevitably internalised is a compacted sense of rejection, failure and unacceptability, often together with an unconscious fear of their own destructiveness and power' (p.272).

Over the following years Marcus demonstrated, in therapy, through his symbolic playing out, the emotional grip his anger had on his life and how it had come to overshadow his thinking about his relationships and his vision or confusion about the future. At a review meeting he described how chaotic his world felt and how difficult it was for him to find space to plan his future, and said somewhat wistfully to a stunned review panel that it was like 'playing chess in the dark'.

His murderous rage, often acted out in therapy sessions, was vividly played out when he chose to play with two of the therapy room's baby dolls. He would begin by sitting on the floor changing their nappies and 'feeding' them with a doll's bottle. Then suddenly – with no warning – he would attack the babies. The assaults were vicious and involved stabbing their imaginary genitals or their eyes or holding them by the legs and smashing them against the walls. Marcus would repeat this sequence many times until it was felt that the 'play' should be stopped because of the acute awareness of a sadistic element beginning to creep into the enactment. It was the moment the quality of the play changed from rage and revenge on the babies to a sense that Marcus was enjoying the 'pain' he was inflicting on the 'babies'. At this point, he was stopped from doing what he was doing, and a discussion ensued about how curious it was that vulnerable babies could evoke in all of us an urge to hurt as if their complete dependence and vulnerability could release fantasies of wanting to crush or bite or punish.

But the key task at that point was to ensure Marcus heard how all people – whatever their circumstances – had similar feelings, and that while it was acceptable to have these perverse feelings or to play out these worrying sensations, it would never to be acceptable to do this outside the therapy room. Of course, in his case, he had very real memories of having to care for his baby brothers and sisters.

Hunter (2001) works with young people and children who have suffered multiple trauma and who have no clear idea of the 'before' and 'after' of the traumatic event. Instead they have developed defences which 'blur and deny painful happenings: they use strategies of distraction, of minimisation, of manic cheerfulness or of placatory passivity' (p.159), some of which can be useful survival skills. However, some become 'rigid defences which prevent good experiences getting through to the child', and because these children are

> out of touch with their experience, it is often visited on others in a particularly nasty way: children who have been beaten can savagely attack a more vulnerable child or an adult at the point of vulnerability. Children who have been denigrated, sexually abused or scapegoated can be vicious bullies as they throw the unwanted experience into anyone who gets emotionally close. (p.159)

Hunter eloquently speaks of the painful and 'hazardous' process that the therapist, and all adults who form the recovery team, have to try to absorb and make sense of, as they contend with what she describes as the various 'reversed repetitions'.

It was intriguing how regularly Marcus used to manipulate any play or movement, to throw an object at a large clock in the therapy room. Invariably the clock would be struck so violently with a ball or bat or any missile at hand, that it would fall to the floor. After a considerable period of time of this repetition, it occurred to the therapist to suggest to Marcus that there was nothing random about this sequence, that there was something about this clock that triggered a resentment in him. Eventually Marcus conceded that he used to watch the clock at his home constantly, desperate for his mother to return and struggling with feelings of being a prisoner, both of the children and his mother. He was battling unconsciously against powerful feelings of wanting to rebel and break free, but with an awareness that he couldn't totally abandon the young children in his care, and the frustration and bitterness this caused him.

Once the clock had been identified for what it symbolized to Marcus, he and the therapist could work within the safety and containment of metaphor, and bombard the clock together, until it fell from the hook. For several minutes it seemed to offer Marcus a forum for giving shape or form to his anger and maybe fear that his parents might never come home – leaving him to try to cope for ever with being responsible for the babies. This opened discussion about how unfair and painful this situation was, and how he deserved a better childhood – one where he might feel free to be a 'normal' child, getting his needs met – rather than a binding arrangement. Within this milieu the loss of Marcus's childhood was mourned. He would often stand with an attitude of a young child saying 'play' in a very childlike voice – which is exactly what he and his therapist did together in the potentially creative space of therapy.

When children begin to engage and play symbolically, their play can become perverse. Mother can become a wild animal who claws and spits and consumes everything in her path. Other times might show a toy 'mother' who would chase her 'child', suddenly changing into an animal figure. A common response to any linking of the acting out to the child's own fears, or attempts to show something of what Cant (2002, p.272) calls an 'internal mother, who could not be relied upon to be trustworthy, but who might turn the world upside-down at any moment in a very frightening way, until bad was good and good was bad' would be denied – or the child would state it was 'only a game'!

Loss of love re-experienced

On one occasion, Marcus chose to lie on a large cushion in the therapy room, curled up in a foetal shape on the cushion, facing away from the therapist. He cried unceasingly for most of the session. The therapist stayed connected to him – and his emotional grieving – with his voice, trying to console him as he wept because he said he truly felt that no one loved him. Although the natural urge as an adult would be to reach out physically and hold a young person in distress, the therapist has to be mindful of the mixed messages this could arouse because of a blurring of the therapy boundaries.

The therapist's primary task is to contain and absorb the outpourings of the child, but not to become the idealized mother figure, who can physically replace the love the child never had. The therapist has to remain clear all the time that it is the child's emotional needs that have to be worked through – and recognize when boundaries 'slip' and suddenly it is the therapist's own, very primitive needs that are surfacing.

Over and above the difficult and controversial issue of touch is another layer in the therapist's professional dilemma. He is alone in a room with a child who has been subjected to physical and often sexual trauma, and has a professional responsibility to ensure the child isn't exposed to a re-traumatization. There is also the unpalatable matter of protection against allegations of sexual malpractice that could be made by the child, if she felt the therapist was becoming too close physically. She might find it sexually arousing, which could lead to further complications or could even trigger an aggressive outburst if she confused a loving interaction with sex and pain. This delicate and extremely difficult dynamic within the therapy room, with this particular group of severely damaged children and adolescents, can pose a very real challenge for many therapists. However, the very nature of the child's abuse demands that we suspend our desire to put all things right for the child. If a situation arises within a session, the therapist has to adhere to the boundaries imposed – for the protection of both of them. A therapist can be just as effective and supportive by using a loving tone of voice and gently encouraging the child to try to make connections between her feelings of falling apart and disintegrating with early memories – but only when ready to do so. There is a consensus that the therapist has to 'sit with the pain' and work with it. There is also a realization that the therapist can offer consolation and a supportive presence just by quietly sitting, occasionally reflecting what the child is projecting in the room and thinking aloud.

The therapist has to be clear all the time that it is the child's emotional needs that have to be worked through, and to know that when boundaries are crossed it is the therapist's own very primitive needs that are surfacing.

Marcus's very real memories were of being left in an adult role to care for very young brothers and sisters in the absence of their real parents. There would have been many times when he would have tried his best to provide nurture and care for the babies, but he was far too young to accept his role as parent. His fear and resentment at having to cope must have given rise to fantasies of wanting to get away from the younger ones, of wanting to get rid of them. Perhaps there were even moments of wanting to murder them when, despite all his efforts, the babies continued to cry, rejecting his efforts to placate them.

In time Marcus discussed his anger and resentment that he had had to sacrifice his own childhood, not only to tend to the basic needs of the babies left in his care but also to allow his parent figures to follow their pleasures or desires. It was indeed an upside-down world where nothing was as it should be.

Marcus eventually linked his deep distrust of adults to his early experiences. His reactions were not dissimilar to those of Matthew, who was nine when Hunter first saw him:

> The brutality that he had experienced was linked in his own mind with occasions when he lost his temper and punched, kicked and tore [at his adoptive carers]. At these moments he seemed to shift from rage that they were saying 'no' to him, to an enactment of brutal uncontrolled aggression. He admitted that he was not sure at some points who was hitting whom. Although he was doing the punching he was overtaken by a vendetta against frustrating adults and his satisfaction in his own power was something he found hard to condemn. He would not accept the fact that he was becoming the bully that he hated. In his mind he needed his defences, he needed his protective rages, he needed to feel in control, he needed to use powerful aggression. The consequences of these defences for his relationships were a price Matthew seemed prepared to pay. (Hunter 2001, p.161)

Bowlby (1979) talks of the child's need for proximity to the body of the mother and the longing for the physical presence of her caregivers, and of her corresponding traumatic experiences of separation and loss. This laid the empirical foundations of his attachment theory. Laschinger (2004) writes:

> The threat of loss leads to anxiety and anger; actual loss to anger and sorrow. When efforts to restore the bond fail, attachment behaviour may diminish, but will persist at an unconscious level and may become reactivated by reminders of the lost adult, or new experiences of loss. (p.xviii)

Body or movement play therapy is based on acute attention to clues given by children, through observation of their body postures, gestures and how they make use of the space that surrounds them. In the case of Sarah (see case example, page 118), she was helped to alter her body image; linking body image to self-image allowed the therapist to observe her growth. Sarah was allowed to regress to a foetal shape by the therapist staying with her, remaining connected by eye contact and speaking to her. He then took responsibility for gently mobilizing her, following through early developmental movements, and bringing her back to her chronological age, stage by stage until she was able to engage in a synchronized movement sequence that involved eye contact and a state of alertness.

Valuable insights into the child's emotional state can be gleaned by correlating qualities of preferred movements or planes – such as the horizontal plane and the need to 'give in' to the floor – with their psychological implications, such as feeling low or giving in to the weight of her body. Feeling depressed appears to be experienced in the body as needing almost to surrender to a desire or need to retreat into the body, into the floor; this was shown by Sarah's foetal shape on the big cushions.

Children need to express their feelings about their bodies and their bodily functions, and about what has happened to them. They may spontaneously express intense feelings when emotions are released during movement or body exercises (James 1989). James stresses how important it is to make them feel comfortable about any such release. Reassurance could come in the form of emphasis on how normal it is for muscles to hold tight for protection, and then release when it seems safe to do so and that when this happens, feelings and memories can emerge during these releases. Therapist and child can play with holding on and letting go and begin to be able to talk about how it feels when the tightening goes and move towards discussing associations the child may make during this interaction.

It is important to mention that, for some children, lying down or the horizontal plane can trigger images of abuse, physical as well as sexual. One 15-year-old girl clearly described being raped by an adolescent in the house where she was being fostered. When recalling this event and playing it out with toy characters, she recalled how cold the floor was, and what she could see on the ceiling. This was detail she would have focused on, rather than the act itself, a clear use of dissociation coming to the aid of her sense of being overwhelmed by the memory of the actual experience. The way she coped with the memory would in time be challenged, and feelings that truly belonged to the act of rape worked through, at a gradual pace and in a way that would address issues of guilt and shame.

On some occasions it may be necessary to become actively involved to enable a child to communicate strong feelings. By engaging physically with the child, the therapist creates a permissive therapeutic tension. Therapist and child can takes turns to roar like a lion. One of the most potent interventions in this work is the ability to match the child's intensity in a containing, controlled way. A large box can be used to great effect when the therapist gives permission to the child to kick the box and, if necessary, to make a hole in the side of the box, if this achieves a safe release of tension.

When children attack the idea of receiving anything good

Some children choose to use their therapy time to make the therapist feel worthless, hopeless and bad, and they persist with the conviction that therapy is a waste of their time. This could be interpreted as the children projecting their own feelings of helplessness onto the therapist. The therapist will hold this in mind, and is also aware that, in spite of their declarations, they still turn up, even if they justify this by saying their key carer 'made' them do so.

Alvarez (1995) described a child she had worked with as 'expert in raising hopes only to dash them again'. One such child might be Tracey.

Tracey was nine years old, with a brother who was also placed at SACCS but not living in the same house. She was making great strides at her mainstream school and making friends there. Overall, she was seen to be progressing well enough for the local authority to be trying to find a foster home for her with a view to possible adoption. Tracey had been affected by the moving on of other children within her house and seemed agitated and tense.

She usually started her therapy session with a loud groan and clear signs of her impatience at the therapist's arrival. Once in the therapy room, she moved swiftly into her role as teacher – a particularly bossy teacher, who is hard to please. Sometimes she would write a word or sentence on the wipe board and then disguise the words by colouring or squiggling over them. The therapist was told to work out what she had written, often a very difficult task. While Tracey watched the therapist struggle to unravel or untangle, she would often jeer or smile trium-phantly if he failed to see behind the camouflaged message. 'Told you. You're useless!' she would exclaim. Any attempt at reflections such as 'I wonder if you really want me to help you unravel some of your muddled thoughts, but think it would be too painful if I actually did so' would be met with an explosion of frustration at the adult's suggestion that she had any muddled thoughts, saying that what he wanted was for her to tell him things about sex, and that nothing had ever happened to her anyway. She would remind the therapist that her mother was beautiful and that the therapist was old, ugly and useless and unable to help her in any meaningful way. Perhaps her deepest fear was that this was true – that no-one could bear to hear her story or be able to help her come to terms with the realities of her earlier life.

On one occasion, Tracey drew a 'portrait' of the therapist – a breast, a face, a bottom and a penis cut off from a body, and positioned in no recognisable ordering, random almost. It was a representation of a person whose body was fragmented and split into many pieces that almost needed cutting out and then reassembling into a recognizable whole person. In effect, Tracey had created a 'body jigsaw'. It seemed to demand a response from the therapist of what he saw in her drawing, and for Tracey to verify if the therapist's interpretation made sense to her. Tracy's reaction was to rip the picture into many pieces, shouting and raging as she did so. At the end of the session, she was told that the therapist was going to gather up the pieces and try to mend the picture again before he saw her for a session the following week. Tracey shrieked that he was mad and that she was dumping it because it was rubbish. The theme of being 'dumped' at SACCS by her mother had been raised before. She was reminded of the policy that any piece of work created or undertaken by a child was kept in her folder and then put in her special draw, however primitive in form; it was certainly never disregarded or casually thrown away.

Between sessions the therapist reassembled and taped together the picture. At the next therapy session, when Tracey reminded the therapist that she had 'rubbished' her picture last week, the mended version was produced. 'What did you do that for?' she responded, her voice incredulous, mocking – but intrigued. When told that anything she produced in the therapy session was important, she reached out for the drawing. For a fleeting moment, she seemed to almost drop her guard, a smile appearing as she gazed at the paper, studiously reassembled. She scanned the therapist's face, making sure he was attending to her, but said nothing. She broke the silence by suddenly and noisily scrunching and ripping at the paper, all the time her eyes firmly fixed on his face as if searching for a reaction to her action. Rather than struggling to remain neutral in the light of the negative symbolization that was being enacted, or looking surprised or shocked, the therapist responded by telling Tracey how hard it must be sometimes to allow anyone to get close, or to hear – or see – that an adult thinks she is special and lovable.

Thus, it can be seen that Tracey's drive to destroy bears out the hypothesis that we outlined above: that some children can attempt to make the therapist feel worthless by projecting on to the therapist their own sense of worthlessness. In Tracey's case, too, what she did seemed to symbolize her need to destroy anything good, as well as her need to see the therapist's own dismay, evoked by her action. This is reminiscent of Cant's observations of a child who 'attacked the possibility of her

receiving anything good. Time and time again, any moments of hope-
fulness, once they were recognised, were destroyed, and destroyed with
glee' (2002, p.274). However, in this case there was hope that perhaps
on some level Tracey had internalized that she had been clearly held in
mind as the therapist showed by having put the picture together. By
doing so he demonstrated that adults were willing and determined to
emotionally contain her feelings of nothingness and moments of feeling
fragmented and disembodied – that even if she now had the last laugh
and the last word ('now it is all ripped again – and this time leave it that
way'), she will have at least experienced a sense of being held, even if
only for a moment.

Sarah: Anger locked in

The first time her therapist met Sarah, she was slumped on a sofa in
the reception area, wearing shoes with enormous heels. Her hair
virtually covered her face, like a veil, obscuring her eyes. She was
laughing very loudly while appearing to be engrossed with her
hair, which she twisted vigorously, yet at the same time clearly
attending to a question her carer was asking her. She stalwartly
avoided making any connection with the therapist, who stood in
front of her introducing himself and suggesting they went
somewhere more quiet where they might discuss the possibility of
undertaking therapy together.

During Sarah's deliberations as to whether she was going to
'give you a go', she left the therapist feeling stranded. But this did
afford the opportunity for Sarah to be observed interacting with
her key carer, with whom she clearly had a comfortable relationship. One question was whether this open display of closeness,
which was amplified by Sarah inclining her body towards the
adult, which effectively blocked out the therapist, was perhaps
serving as a physical defence, to support Sarah's discomfort at the
prospect of meeting a new therapist. Perhaps she felt it was the

therapist's turn to feel awkward, and she certainly felt disinclined to 'rescue' him.

As if waking from a reverie, Sarah turned towards the therapist in a surprisingly fluid motion and planted her impressive heels firmly into the ground. It was only at that moment that she glanced up – fleetingly – into his face. Her eyes were an astonishing hue of light blue, and they made the swiftest connection before reverting to their downcast focus. Using both her hands to dig into the sofa, she heaved her body to her feet, emitting a grunting sound. She was surprisingly tall for a 14-year-old and, indeed, she seemed to overpower the therapist as they finally squared up to each other.

With a dismissive glance, Sarah walked ahead to the therapy room. The apparent casualness of their walking off together was in sharp contrast to the anxiety injected into the meeting. Sarah's entire pelvic region was acutely held in a contracted position, much the same as if she had been punched in the stomach. The way her body posture held her pelvis impacted on the way she carried her body. It had the visual effect of pressing down on her legs, which bent at the knee, giving the impression of being drawn down, at the same time giving the observer the feeling that she was unstable, that she could easily fall backwards. As she walked, her body gave off a sense of vulnerability or being precariously balanced.

Movement analysis informed by psychological understanding suggests that the way Sarah's body stressed the horizontal plane indicates a lack of autonomy and confidence, as opposed to an emphasis on the more 'up–down' vertical plane as in a more buoyant walk, which could strike an observer as someone who was confident and self-assured.

After many sessions with a child, a movement profile can add insights into a child's emotional state, due to the theoretically close relationship of body and mind. Sexual and physical abuse happen to the body, and by gradually understanding a child's non-verbal communications and meanings, and by mirroring a child's walk, movements and postures, it is possible to access a very real sense of what it is like to be in the child's body. This is gaining a 'kinaesthetic sense' of the child and can produce a powerful counter-transference.

When, in a session, Sarah removed her shoes, her toes on both feet were shown to be curled over in a flexed, claw-like shape, rather than extended. She maintained this posture when she walked. When Sarah and therapist walked together, the therapist copied the way Sarah held in her pelvis and he forced his toes into the same shape as hers. The distortion he felt in his body was extreme, and he felt as if his body was locked with tension. Little wonder, then, that Sarah's pattern when arriving at the therapy room was to drop onto four large cushions and curl into a foetal-like shape. It was reminiscent of someone who had recently subjected herself to a very long and arduous journey and was exhausted physically and mentally. It would also be feasible to suggest the apparent need for Sarah to give in to the floor or cushions, and allow herself to 'indulge' in passive weight. She gave the impression of wanting the cushions to support her, almost to cradle her, but this need also had an emotional link with giving in to a state as if she was depressed.

Once on the cushions, she found it infinitely difficult to find the energy to motivate herself to leave the safety of a symbolic nest. The task of the therapist was to find a way to mobilize Sarah and imbue her with the desire to come out of her place of emotional retreat from everything that overwhelmed her, and to bring her into the present.

What was known of Sarah gave an explanation for how she held herself. For her, a game of hide-and-seek had taken on a terrifying twist. She would run away from her father and try to find a place to hide from him. She was quite clear that discovery meant being severely beaten; it was, therefore, imperative that she find a very good hiding place. It was documented that on occasions she could not achieve this, and neither had she been able to outrun her father when she had been 'found' by him. Sarah was full of deflected anger with her body (specifically her legs) for failing her. However desperate her flight, her body had let her down.

For a long period of time, the therapy concentrated on Sarah rebuilding her belief in her body, forgiving it for failing her and turning this around, so that she could assign blame where it belonged – with her father. The strategy of building up her self-esteem and turning her vulnerability into a confident body image focused on grounding her (literally in a sense) by encouraging her to become physically in touch with the ground. Movement sequences gradually built to kick-boxing, stamping, pounding – and laughter.

It was to be a long time before Sarah's self-image was positive enough to allow her to voice her displaced anger at her father, rather than embody the feeling and turn it in upon herself. In every way, this was easier and even less painful than acknowledging that her father had acted sadistically towards her, a vulnerable child, whatever was in his mind, and had consistently overpowered her in his need to control others.

Exercises

1. Look up at the sky on a cloudy day. Can you find shapes that look like an animal, a person, a monster?

2. Find a piece of fabric and drop it on the floor. What is the first image you see when you look at the fabric?

3. With another person, draw a squiggle on a piece of paper. Ask the other person to add lines to turn the squiggle into a recognisable image. Now, ask the other person to draw a squiggle and you add lines to create a recognisable image. Discuss the images as you draw.

CHAPTER 8

A Framework
for Recovery Assessment

According to Cant (2002), each child placed should be 'held in mind and in body, securely, reliably and consistently' (p.267). This is an essential, indispensable part of the process towards recovery. But how can we assess recovery? SACCS has developed a framework for assessing children's needs and developing recovery plans to meet those needs. This framework is now the glue that binds the integrated approach together.

The recovery assessment is an internal strategy that draws together different professionals and gives priority to (and, by so doing, enhances) the sharing of their information and insights.

Everyone concerned with the child's recovery convenes every six months at a meeting chaired by an independent senior practitioner. Those in the three parts that make up the integrated approach – therapy, life story and therapeutic parenting – are asked to score or scale the child, independently of each other; the areas under observation represent six areas of functioning, on which trauma has had a direct or indirect impact.

Twenty-four objectives for recovery or outcomes for development have been identified. If achieved they would positively indicate a child's recovery to emotional and physical health, and her potential to achieve to her full potential in all aspects of her life. These objectives are grouped together under the areas of:

- learning
- physical development
- emotional development
- attachment
- identity and social development
- communicative development.

The scoring for each section explores the impact of the child's early trauma and early attachment relationships and tracks each child's emotional journey towards reaching her potential for recovery. The scores are transferred to a chart for analysis and comparison with previous assessments. This method of plotting a child's progress avoids drift and helps staff to focus more clearly if they need to come up with new strategies to help the child move forward. Team members alert everyone to any blocks encountered that may be impeding progress. Any new behaviours or any new information that has come to light recently is communicated and woven into the proposed strategy of interventions. Staff are encouraged to use the meetings to present their own feelings and views about the child. They might, for example, discuss the impact the child has on them, living in the same space; or they might think about the impact the child might currently have on the other children in the house where she has been placed.

Staff are able to talk about their struggle to absorb the bombardment of powerful projections they receive from the child and how they interpret their counter-transference. Matters like envy or resentment between team roles can be aired. Feelings of being attacked either mentally or physically can be shared with the group and their support sought if they are experiencing feelings of exhaustion or ambivalence.

The six-monthly meeting, then, is a potential space for staff to increase their understanding of the child and develop plans to help achieve positive outcomes. (This opportunity for the recovery team to think together is in addition to staff consultation with external consultants from the fields of psychotherapy, psychology and psychiatry. Together this and the consultation combine to help the team with their primary task of making connections and emotional links for the child, and being able to get closer to the complexities of the child's internal world.)

Following the assessment each part of the recovery team will create a plan for the next six months' work with the child. In doing this, the therapist may consider the following questions:

- What exactly is the therapist currently doing in a creative therapy session with the sexually abused child? What are the recurring themes?

- How does the therapist feel this is affecting the child? To what extent is it changing the child, if at all? What can the therapist do to support further change or work through blocks if they exist?

- If there seems to be positive change in therapy, why might this be happening?

The recovery assessments and ensuing plans allow the child's recovery to unfold systematically at her own pace. As has been demonstrated throughout this book, the recovery process for highly traumatized and sexually abused children is complex and needs considerable time. The recovery plan is continually reviewed to ensure that the team track the child's progress towards recovery. As Alvarez (1992) reminds us:

Recovery can be a long, slow process, particularly for the children who have been abused chronically at a young age. Disclosure should lead to protection from abuse, but the treatment, and for that matter the disclosure itself, may be undertaken with a child who has hardly got a notion of non-abuse. The child may not share society's feeling that something is changed and resolved by the disclosure. (p.151)

The integrated model

The integrated model contains key aspects that underpin the assessment process:

- Lines of communication between all staff must be open and clearly defined.

- Communications should flow between residential carers, the therapist and life story workers. In addition, all members of the child's recovery team should regularly appraise, update and share with the referring local authority new insights, strategies or anxieties that may occur between reviews or designated contact visits. But due to the damage that children in residential care have often undergone, and the subsequent disturbance that they experience, such communication can be both challenging and exhausting.

- Teachers at the child's school should be very much involved and brought up to date with significant events, behavioural changes or any issue that carers or therapist feel will affect the child's ability to think and contribute to her school life.

- Communication and thinking should be very detailed. A seemingly unimportant comment from a child can often, when placed in a wider context, together with other people's information and insights, make sense in a way it could never do when it was only an isolated utterance.

- Primarily, the task of the life story team is to act as therapeutic detectives and find out about the child's life.

- The recovery team will piece together what is currently known about a child, following subsequent discoveries unearthed by the life story team, including sharing any new interview with a significant person in the child's life.

- The recovery team meets regularly to discuss each child and to probe and debate facts and held beliefs.

- Recovery assessments offer another forum for the combined team to ask questions about the child and develop a shared language and process a way of working with the child to achieve her maximum potential to recover.

- The recovery team think about the child together in order to understand the child better and consider the impact of her trauma on the six areas of functioning.

- The child's stage of emotional development should be identified.

- Integrated working provides a team with a means of tracking progress or highlighting areas of major concern if the child's scores slip.

- Integrated working identifies blocks and looks to other members of the team to offer fresh insights or suggestions for strategies in order to move the child forward.

- The child's internal working model should be analysed, along with what impact this will have had on how the child views herself as well as her relationship with the world around her.

- Strategies, beliefs and interventions should be evaluated.

- A consensus should be reached regarding what works and what does not.

- Integrated working offers a potentially creative space for any member of the recovery team to air or float feelings that the child evokes in them.

- The impact of living with the child should be discussed, and how it feels to have to survive the bombardment of a child's negative projections.

- 'There should be a culture of inquiry which will foster life, creative and containing work.' (Flynn 1998, p.167)

Menzies-Lyth (1988) says that all adults working with children referred to residential care need to be able to absorb 'powerful projections' from them, think about them (together with other staff) and 'return the projections in a more benign state'.

CHAPTER 9

Ending and New Beginnings

No one's story is ever ended, and children who have come through therapy are not at the end of their story but moving from one chapter to another. They will have absorbed the experiences which therapy has helped them to face along with others in their lives. One hopes that therapy will have contributed to the child's recovery; the child will have internalized her experiences; she will have gained a greater understanding of herself and others, becoming more fully integrated; and she will have moved from insecure to secure attachments, able to enjoy healthy relationships with others. She will now be able to make more sense of her life and what happened to her and her own part in it. Confusion will have been replaced by understanding, and rage, fear and anger will no longer overshadow her. The disorder, pain and chaos of the child's earlier life will be behind her but remain a part of her, and her future will be one of potential and promise.

It is important, therefore, that when therapy comes to an end, the therapist should realize that the ending itself is important and should be positive. However, while the positive outcomes just mentioned will have equipped the child better to live her life, that does not mean that ending is easily done. Lanyardo (2004) makes a useful analogy between ending therapy and when a parent lets go of a child so that she can develop and grow, which, she opines, is something needed in both the large and small steps of life. She implies that these parent–child endings are not always easy:

The counterbalancing processes of holding and letting go need to be addressed so that a point is reached where ending therapy acquires the quality of 'a page in life' being turned. This is where the idea of 'transitions' rather than stark beginnings and endings can be helpful. In ordinary life, progressions cannot take place without letting go of something – whether this be the infant letting go of the breast, or letting go of the side of the pool and realising that they really can float or swim. The reality is that developmental processes do not take place in isolation. Beginnings and endings belong together and remain essentially paradoxical in nature. And yet if the idea of, and capacity to tolerate, paradox during a transition can be maintained there is a richness of experience which compensates for the anxieties that change inevitably brings to the inner world. (p.117)

Thus, ending is as important as what went before and the therapist's task has not ended until he and the child say goodbye. Before that the child can be helped to look back to real achievement, growth and maturity. The abuse children have been subjected to and the pain that they have had to face to overcome their adversity would try the hardiest adult. Thus, helping the child to reflect on what she has done, what her achievement has been, is an important part of the therapy task, and one that, so to speak, prepares her for her new life.

The child has not been passive or a passenger in the journey through therapy. There are matters, small and everyday to many of us, that can mean so much to this child. For example, she is now able to invite a hug from the therapist and other adults. This is no small thing when she has been conditioned, through past experience, to regard gestures of apparent affection as laden with sexual potential or threat, when adults were people whose motives were self-interested, when being with them meant having sex with them, and when 'love' was not something which was life-enhancing and affirming but involved pain, shame, confusion and destructiveness.

The child needs to experience the ending as significant, and just as the therapist must let the child go, so must the child let the therapist go –

the child's part in the ending is no more passive than it has been during the therapy. Child and therapist may have mixed feelings about the end. The child may wonder why therapy is ending when she has become used to it after so much resistance to starting it, while the therapist may feel a sense of loss.

The therapist may also have a genuine concern for the future: he may realize that the child's life may still be a difficult one as she grows to maturity, allied with his knowledge that therapy in later life, if required, may not be easily available. Thus, what has occurred between child and therapist may be the last, best chance for the child. However, the child's experiences in therapy may have given her the awareness to avoid negative and destructive relationships in the future, and to seek out positive relationships that will help her.

Ending will be 'the complicated mix of anger, sadness, pain and regret, the inevitable feelings of there being so much left that is incomplete' (Lanyardo, 1992, p.120), which will be balanced by what has been achieved and what there is to come. Endings and beginnings run simultaneously and that the whole process can be thought of as another transition in life, something through which we move, rather than stopping at one point and starting at another.

There are questions to be asking when thinking about ending therapy: What progress has been made? What healing has taken place? What is the difference in the child now from when she entered therapy? Has enough been done to allow the child to be let go with the possibility of further growth and recovery? How able is she to face the world? Other questions will look further ahead, for example: What kind of contact would be appropriate after therapy? Are follow-ups helpful? For a child in care, the therapist may become an important figure in her new landscape and contact may help to augment what has been gained.

Many children leave therapy and go into family placement, a transition where the therapist's skills and knowledge are essential. This can be a time of waiting and introductions, where recovery continues and action is taken to ensure that children are placed with families who are most suitable. An integral part of this is ensuring that the child is ready for placement, and the therapist, alongside the life story worker, key carer and family placement worker, will work together to support the child during the transition.

The child who is ready for placement will have the capacity to separate and move away and the therapist's role will be to help this to happen. This does not mean that there will not be a need for therapy in the future; there might be. Such a need will be determined through the application of the assessment process in foster care.

A child's departure should be planned and structured around a series of events – for example, saying goodbye to the therapist, to the key carer, to other children, and going to a new life in a placement – each stage requires its own planning. The therapist is in a good position to advise about the child's strengths and the kind of placement required and what can be expected of her in the placement. It is important that the child's expectations are managed and that those working with her are aware that further upheaval may lead to a situation where she may not think it worth making the emotional investment required in moving on. This could be potentially disastrous: a child who has come through therapy requires stability and assurance, not a return to a common pattern of moving from one place to another, something which both her family and the care system may have perpetuated in the past .

The therapist's role during the transition is also to be supportive to the child, and not to miss clues to anything about which she may feel uneasy despite outward appearances to the contrary. Children at this juncture may be emotionally fragile and may not be able to say exactly what they are thinking, or may not have the confidence to voice their reservations and unease. Thus, a child who spends a day with a potential foster family and is uneasy about it may not say so in so many words but might, for example, say that she did not like the food she was offered in the home. One of the signals a therapist should be alert to is an indication that while the child is not expressing anxiety or reservations, she may want to sabotage the placement.

The therapist, with others, has an important role in handling the child's worries, anxieties and fantasies, and in helping her resolve the

conflicts she feels about moving on, letting go, attachment and separation. It is very important that the therapist, as a core member of the
recovery team, helps hold the child and keep her safe at this time of transition.

When the child and therapist say goodbye it will be a significant
thing for both of them. They have developed a relationship, where the
child's greatest fears have been expressed, worst experiences revealed,
and most painful memories brought to the surface. It may well be one of
the most intimate relationship that the child will ever experience. It is
also one that has enabled her to come out of depths in a way she would
not have imagined possible. Thus, no matter how well it is handled, it
will create a void. The therapist needs to think carefully about how he
will do this and rehearse it. It is not something that should be done
suddenly and without preparation or warning; there should be no
sudden shocks or surprises. Indeed, some advance warning to the child is
advisable. The therapist might, for example, want to make a point of
saying that in, say, three months' time they won't be seeing one another
again. There needs to be Winnicott's 'potential space' for thinking. It is,
as we said, a time for positive reflection.

While the therapist helps the child to look back with pride on what
she has achieved, where she has come from and where she is now, he
should also acknowledge some of his own feelings. He may want to
emphasize that though they are parting and may not be meeting again,
he will not forget her, that she will be missed, and that he hopes that she
realizes that. He may say that there are, say, 12 more sessions and ask her
what she would like to do in that time.

Lanyardo (2004) says that even when therapy has gone well the
ending may be conflicted and undermine the positive outcomes of the
therapy. She places high on the list of desirable qualities in the therapeutic process what she calls 'the good enough ending'. She notes that it is
important for the therapist to avoid the conclusion of therapy adding to
or repeating the other traumatic separations the child may have suffered.
It is very valuable for the child to see the end of the relationship as a
positive step.

The lives, outlook and perceptions of an abused child have been distorted. Therapy has helped to restore a more healthy perspective. The child is no longer imprisoned by her past but will be able to make her own decisions. She is better equipped to deal with life, she is able to avoid some of the pitfalls of the past, and she has warnings about dangers that can lie ahead. Therapy offers some of the tools that allow us to work at life's problems.

The 'good enough' ending in therapy is not dissimilar to those endings which parents understand very well, and the outcome can be the same for the child who has been in therapy. She comes to her new life with a realization that life can be a series of beginnings, which result from simultaneous endings, and an experience of almost perpetual renewal due to our ability to absorb, process and learn from our experiences.

Exercise

1.   Lanyardo compared ending therapy to letting go of a child (see p.125). If you have children, describe how you felt when you had to let each of them cope with their first day at school. Remember your feelings on your own first day at school. (see Question 1 on p.56). How might these feelings have affected how you felt about leaving your children? How did each child cope with the separation?

Notes

1. Children can split a team. This can happen because if the team is unified and working together the child will test its ability to continue working with her in a positive way. One way she will do this is by trying to cause difficulties within the team, playing one person off against the other, so that the team becomes divided and split. For the child to feel safe enough to trust the team she will need to see that the team is capable of surviving her attempts to split them.

   Also, children who have been severely damaged in early childhood have major difficulties in holding on to any difficult feelings (for example, aggression or anger) and they will try to get rid of these feelings by projecting them onto certain team members. They will then fear that the person who is now holding the child's 'split off' feelings will attack them in some way, as they are now full of angry, aggressive, bad feelings. In an attempt to create some safety, the child will preserve other team members as good, caring and protective people. So, in the same way that the child has split off her bad feelings and kept only the good, the team is now split into two – good and bad. The aim in treatment is to enable the child to move to a position where she can hold on to both good and bad, positive and negative feelings within herself, and to be able to see this same thing in those that care for her.

2. Those wanting an engrossing survey of the changing understanding of childhood are referred to Lloyd deMause's magisterial work *The History of Childhood* (1976), London: Souvenir Press.

3. Fifteen is given here as being the year below that of sexual consent. A child or young person aged 15 and under cannot by law consent to sex. Obviously, above 16 there is such a thing as non-consensual sex, and people of any age can be sexually abused.

4. ChildLine's estimate may well be correct, but it is wise to remember that girls outnumber boys in calling the helpline on almost any subject by a ratio of 4:1, something which may skew the figures. However, given that males are less likely to report sexual abuse, anyway, it is likely that other estimates would indicate the same proportions.

5. For a discussion of concepts of family and other relationships for abused children, see Rose, R. and Philpot, T. (2004) *The Child's Own Story: Life Story Work with Traumatized Children.* London: Jessica Kingsley Publishers.

6. For a summary of recent research see Glaser, D. (2001) 'Child abuse, neglect and the brain: A review', *Journal of Child Psychology and Psychiatry and Allied Disciplines 41,* 1, 97–116; and Balbernie, R. (2001) 'Circuits and circumstances: The neurobiological consequences of early relationship experiences and how they shape later behaviour', *Journal of Child Psychotherapy 27,* 3, 237–255.

7. When the bond affects kidnap victims or hostages so that they develop positive feelings towards those on whom they have come to depend in this way, this is most commonly called Stockholm syndrome.

References

Aiyegbusi, A. (2004) 'Touch and the impact of trauma in therapy relationships with adults.' In K. White (ed.) *Touch: Attachment and the Body*. London: Karnac Books.

Alvarez, A. (1992) *Live Company: Psychoanalytic Psychotherapy with Autistic, Borderline, Deprived and Abused Children*. London: Routledge.

Alvarez, A. (1995) 'Motiveless malignity.' *Journal of Child Psychotherapy 21*, 2, 163–182.

Archer, C. (2003) 'Weft and warp: Developmental impact of trauma and implications for healing.' In C. Archer and A. Burnell (eds) *Trauma, Attachment and Family Permanence: Fear Can Stop You Loving*. London: Jessica Kingsley Publishers.

Bannister, A. (2003) *Creative Therapies with Traumatized Children*. London: Jessica Kingsley Publishers.

Bion, W. (1989) *Learning from Experience*. London: Routledge.

Bowlby, J. (1969) *Attachment and Loss: Vol .1: Attachment*. London: Hogarth Press.

Bowlby, J. (1979) *The Making and Breaking of Affectional Bonds*. London: Tavistock.

Boyle, S. (1997), 'Introduction.' In M. Bray *Sexual Abuse: The Child's Voice – Poppies in the Rubbish Heap*. London: Jessica Kingsley Publishers.

Bray. M. (1997) *Sexual Abuse: The Child's Voice – Poppies in the Rubbish Heap*. London: Jessica Kingsley Publishers.

Brier, J.N. (1992) *Child Abuse Trauma: Theory and Treatment of the Lasting Effects*. Newbury Park, CA: Sage.

Browne, A. and Finkelhor, D. (1986) 'Impact of child sexual abuse: A review of the research.' *Psychological Bulletin 99*, 1, 66–67.

Burnell, A. and Archer, C. (2003) 'Setting up the loom: Attachment theory revisited.' In C. Archer and A. Burnell (eds) *Trauma, Attachment and Family Permanence: Fear Can Stop You Loving*. London: Jessica Kingsley Publishers.

Cairns, K. (2002) *Attachment, Trauma and Resilience: Therapeutic Caring for Children*. London: BAAF Adoption and Fostering.

Cant, D. (2002) '"Joined-up psychotherapy": The place of individual psychotherapy in residential therapeutic provision for children.' *Journal of Child Psychotherapy 28*, 3, 267–281.

Carozza, P.M. and Hierstiener, C.L. (1982) 'Young female incest victims in treatment: Stages of growth seen with a group art therapy model.' *Clinical Social Work Journal 10*, 3, 165–175.

Caviston, P. (2004) 'Is love all it takes?' *YoungMinds Magazine* January/February, p.000.

Chethik, M. (2000) *Techniques of Child Therapy: Psychodynamic Strategies*. New York: Guilford Press.

ChildLine (2003) *Annual Report*. London: ChildLine.

Children's Hours Trust (2002) *Children's Hours: Listening Creatively to Children*. Burgess Hill: Children's Hours Trust.

Cody, M. (1987) 'Art therapy within a general hospital paediatric unit. Images and enactment in childhood.' Conference proceedings.

Cohen, D. (2002) *How the Child's Mind Develops*. Hove: Routledge.

Connor, T., Sclare I., Dunbar, D. and Elliffe, I. (1985) 'Making a life story book.' *Adoption and Fostering 9*, 2.

Davis, M. and Wallbridge, D. (1991) *Boundary and Space. An Introduction to the Work of D.W. Winnicott*. London: Karnac Books.

Department of Health (2003) *Safeguarding Children: What to Do If You Are Worried a Child is Being Abused*. London: Department of Health.

Department for Education and Skills (2005) *Referrals, Assessments, and Children and Young People on the Child Protection Registers, England – Year ending 31 March 2004*. London: Department for Education and Skills.

Erikson, E.H. (1965) *Childhood and Society* (revised edition). London: Hogarth Press.

Flynn, D. (1998) 'In-patient Work in a Therapeutic Community.' In M. Lanyado and A. Horne (eds) *The Handbook of Child and Adolescent Psychotherapy: Psychoanalytic Approaches*. London: Routledge.

Gerhardt, S. (2004) *Why Love Matters: How Affection Shapes a Baby's Brain*. Hove: Brunner-Routledge.

Gregory, J. (2004) *Sickened: The Memoir of a Munchausen by Proxy Childhood*. London: Century.

Guardian, The (2005) 'Vital statistics: The world of women in numbers.' 19 May.

Hadamard, J. (1954) *The Psychology of Invention in a Mathematical Field*. London: Dover Publications.

Hermon, J.L. (1992) *Trauma and Recovery*. New York: Basic Books.

Horne, A. (1999) 'Normal Emotional Development.' In A. Horne and M. Lanyado (eds) *Handbook of Child and Adolescent Psychotherapy: Psychoanalytical Approaches*. London: Routledge.

Howe, D. (2000) 'Attachment theory.' In M. Davies (ed.) *The Blackwell Encyclopaedia of Social Work*. Oxford: Blackwell.

Hunter, M. (2001) *Psychotherapy with Young People in Care: Lost and Found*. Hove: Brunner-Routledge.

James, B. (1989) *Teching Traumatized Children: New Insights and Creative Interverntions*. New York: The Free Press.

James, B. (1994) *Handbook for Treatment of Attachment-Trauma Problems in Children*. New York: The Free Press.

Kahr, B. (ed.) (2002) *Within The Legacy of Winnicott: Essays on Infant and Child Mental Health Development*. London: Karnac Books.

Karr-Morse, R. and Wiley, M. (1997) *Ghosts from the Nursery: Tracing the Roots of Violence*. New York: Atlantic Monthly Press.

Kelley, S.J. (1984) 'The use of art therapy with sexually abused children.' *Journal of Psycho-social Nursing, 22* 12, 12–18.

Kübler-Ross, E. (1970) *On Death and Dying*. London: Tavistock.

Laschinger, B. (2004) 'Attachment Theory and The John Bowlby Memorial Lecture: A Short History.' In K. White (ed.) *Touch: Attachment and the Body*. London: Karnac.

Levy, T.M. and Orlans, M.(1998) *Attachment, Trauma and Healing: Understanding and Treating Attachment Disorder in Children and Families*. Washington, DC: CWLA Press.

Meekums, B. (2002) *Dance Movement Therapy.* London: Sage.

Menzies-Lyth, J. (1988) 'Containing anxiety in institutions.' In *Selected Essays Vol 1.* London: Free Association Books.

Miller, A. (1995) *The Drama of Being a Child* (revised edition). London: Virago.

Murphy, J. (1998) 'Art therapy with sexually abused children and young people.' *Inscape 3,* 1, 10–16.

Oremland, J. (1998) 'Play, dreams and creativity: Psychoanalytic study of the child.' *Techniques of Child Therapy: Psychodynamic Strategies 53,* 84–93.

Perry, B., Pollard, R., Blakely, T., Baker, W. and Vigilante, D. (1995) 'Childhood trauma, the neurobiology of adaptation and the use of development of the brain: How states become traits.' *Infant Mental Health Journal 16,* 4, 271–291.

Piaget, J. (1951) *Play, Dreams and Imitation in Childhood.* London: Routledge.

Plaut, E. (1979) 'Play and adaptation.' *Psychoanalytic Study of the Child 34,* 217–232.

Plotnikoff, J. and Wolfson, R. (2005) *In Their Own Words: The Experiences of 50 Young Witnesses in Criminal Proceedings.* London: NSPCC.

Poincaré, H. (1982) *Foundations of Science.* Washington, DC: University Press of America.

Prior, S. (1996) *Object Relations in Severe Trauma: Psychotherapy of the Sexually Abused Child.* Northvale, NJ and London: John Aronson.

Revell, P. (2003) 'Slipping through the net.' *The Guardian,* 14 October.

Richardson, A.J. and Montgomery, P. (2005) 'The Oxford-Durham study: A randomised controlled trial of dietary supplementation with fatty acids in children with developmental co-ordination disorder.' *Pediatrics 115,* 1300–1366.

Rose, R. and Philpot, T. (2004) *The Child's Own Story: Life Story Work with Traumatized Children.* London: Jessica Kingsley Publishers.

Sagar, C. (1990) 'Working with Cases of Child Sexual Abuse. In C. Case and T. Dalley (eds) *Working with Children in Art Therapy.* London and New York: Routledge.

Sanderson, C. (2004) *The Seduction of Children: Empowering Parents and Teachers to Protect Children from Child Sexual Abuse.* London: Jessica Kingsley Publishers.

Shengold, L. (1988) 'Play and therapeutic action.' *Psychoanalytic Study of the Child 11,* 2, 146–151.

Siegel, D. (2003) 'An interpersonal neurobiology of psychotherapy.' In M. Solomon and D. Siegel (eds) *Healing Trauma.* New York: W.W. Norton & Company.

Stember, C. (1980) 'A new use in the diagnosis and treatment of sexually abused children.' In *Art Therapy: Sexual Abuse of Chidren: Selected Readings.* Washington, DC: US Department of Health.

Sutton-Smith, B. and Herron, R.E. (1971) *Child's Play.* New York and Chichester: Wiley.

Tomlinson, P. (2004) *Therapeutic Approaches in Work with Traumatized Children and Young People: Theory and Practice.* London: Jessica Kingsley Publishers.

Trevarthen, M.E. (2001) 'Setting the scene. A window to childhood.' Paper given to the 7th Professional Conference of the UK Council for Psychotherapy, 7 September.

Van der Kolk, B.A. and Greenberg, M.S. (1987) *The Psychobiology of Trauma Response: Hyperarousal, Constriction and Addiction to Traumatic Re-exposure in Post Traumatic Stress Disorder. A Psychological and Biological Sequalae.* Washington, DC: American Psychiatric Press.

Wilson, P. (1999) 'Therapy and consultation in residential care.' In A. Horne and M. Lanyado (eds) *Handbook of Child and Adolescent Psychotherapy: Psychoanalytic Approaches.* London: Routledge.

Winnicott, D.W. (1965) *The Maturational Processes and the Facilitating Environment: Studies in the Theory of Emotional Development.* London: Hogarth Press and the Institute of Psycho-Analysis.

Winnicott, D.W, (1968) 'Playing: It's theoretical status in the clinical situation.' *International Journal of Psycho-Analysis 49,* 591–599.

Winnicott, D.W. (1971) *Playing and Reality.* Harmondsworth: Penguin.

Young, L. (1992) 'Sexual abuse and the problem of embodiment.' *Child Abuse and Neglect 16,* 1, 89–100.

YoungMinds (2004) *Mental Health in Infancy.* London: YoungMinds.

Ziegler, D. (2002) *Traumatic Experience and the Brain: A Handbook for Understanding and Treating Those Traumatized as Children.* Phoenix, AZ: Acacia Publishing.

The Story of SACCS

Sexual abuse was at one time most commonly referred to as incest and was thought to occur only in isolated pockets. In the 1960s and 1970s it began to emerge as the battered baby syndrome. Until then the early professional agendas had tended to concentrate very much on physical abuse and neglect, but then a series of official inquiries, resulting from scandals, brought it very much to the fore in the minds of professionals, the public and the media.

The challenge in the early 1980s for the social worker in child protection was to deal with this new phenomenon as part of everyday practice. Social workers had to develop new skills to communicate with children on a subject which they, as adults, had difficulty with, that is talking about sex and their own sexuality, and, moreover, doing this in a way that could withstand the rigours of legal scrutiny.

It was at this point that Mary Walsh, now Chief Executive of SACCS, got together with a colleague, Madge Bray, who was working to help disturbed children communicate by using toys. Together, they looked at how they could adapt the use of the toy box to help this very vulnerable group of children communicate their distress, especially about the abuse they had suffered. Above all, they wanted to give children a voice in decisions that would be made about them, particularly in court.

SACCS comes into being

Working within the culture of uncertainty and confusion that prevailed at the time, Mary Walsh and Madge Bray became disenchanted at the lack of time and resources available to do this work properly. They saw no alternative: in January 1987 they took it upon themselves to meet the profound needs of the deeply traumatized children whom they were seeing every day and who found themselves effectively lost and without any influence on their futures.

SACCS came into being in Madge Bray's back bedroom – the typewriter had to be unplugged to use the photocopier! Demand for the venture on which they were now embarked soon became apparent: they were inundated with requests to see children and help them to communicate about their distress. Mary Walsh and Madge Bray worked with children all over the country, helping them to tell their stories, giving comfort and allowing them to express their pain. They also acted as advocate for children in court and other decision-making bodies, and as case consultants to local authorities. Through this process, as expected, they began to notice that many of the children were changing and beginning to find some resolution to their difficulties.

They also became aware that there were some very small children who, because of what had happened to them, were either too eroticized or too disturbed to be placed in foster care. Many foster carers who were not prepared or trained to deal with very challenging situations day-to-day would quickly become weighed down by the child's sexualized behaviour, and the placement would break down. The real cause of these breakdowns was never acknowledged and, therefore, never dealt with. In time these children were labelled as unfosterable and placed in residential care along with adolescents on remand.

Leaps and Bounds

The heartbreak of watching this happen to three-, four- and five-year-old children was unacceptable. The need was to be able to hold the children and their behaviour lovingly, while they were helped to understand and deal with the root cause of their behaviour. The result was the setting up of Leaps and Bounds, SACCS' first residential care provision.

The birth was a long and difficult one, but after three years the first house, Hopscotch, was opened. It filled up immediately, and the children were cared for by staff trained to understand the issues and encouraged to put love into everything they did.

Many of the children placed in Leaps and Bounds had experienced many placement breakdowns; some had been placed for adoption that had subsequently failed; most had incoherent life histories; some had lost touch with members of their family; and one child, incredibly, had acquired the wrong name. The great need was to find all of this information that was lost in the system, and so the life story service came into existence, to help to piece together the fabric of the children's lives and give them back their own identity.

In addition, a team of professional play therapists was engaged to work with the children in Hopscotch, and subsequently at the new houses – Somersault, Cartwheel, Handstand, Leapfrog and others – while continuing to bring the special SACCS approach to children who were not in residential care.

Within SACCS, all those charged with responsibility for the wellbeing of the child were (and are) expected to share information with each other, so that the whole team holds the child's reality and care.

SACCS Family Placement

The expectation at SACCS was that when children had come to terms with what had happened to them and were ready to move on, their local authorities would find foster families for them. This proved not to be the case in many instances, and children who had worked hard to recover and desperately wanted to be part of a family would have their hopes dashed. As a result their behaviour deteriorated, and it was extremely difficult to watch this happening, especially as the next part of the work needed to be done within a family.

Leaps and Bounds was never intended to become a permanent placement for the children, so looking for potential foster families and training them to care for this very challenging and vulnerable group of children became the responsibility of SACCS Family Placement (originally called Find Us, Keep Us), the fostering and family placement arm of SACCS.

Flying Colours

In 1997 Flying Colours was opened. It was a new project designed to meet the needs of young adolescents. Often these were children who had been traumatized when they were very young, but had only just started to talk about it.

As a therapist, Mary Walsh had worked with many such young people who were not being held in a safe and contained holding environment. She knew that they often ran away when feelings overwhelm them, and sometimes end up living hand to mouth on inner city streets, involved in prostitution, drug taking and worse. Flying Colours offered these young people the same loving and nurturing therapeutic care as the younger children in Leaps and Bounds, while at the same time meeting their different developmental needs

SACCS Care

In 2003 a major rationalization was undertaken to integrate all of the SACCS services which had evolved since the organization's early days. A new company, SACCS Care, was formed, with an organizational focus on the parenting aspect of therapeutic care. This is arguably the most important job carried out with children, some of whom have similar developmental profiles to the most dangerous adults in our society. SACCS believes that unless this issue is addressed properly, traumatized children cannot have a positive experience of parenting, and when the time comes will be unable to parent their own children appropriately.

Today and tomorrow

SACCS is differentiated by a unique integrated model of therapeutic parenting, play therapy, life story work and education support individually tailored to meet children's needs, coupled with a fostering service for those who are ready to move to a family.

At the time of writing, SACCS is a growing Midlands-based organization looking after 50 children and employing 175 professional care staff and managers. The SACCS model is underpinned by a complex structure of practice training and clinical supervision, and these standards of excellence have positioned the organization as a national leader in therapeutic care and recovery.

There are many children outside SACCS struggling with the enormous trauma caused by abuse and neglect, children whose experience has taught them that families are dangerous places in which to live. SACCS believes that every child has a right to the expert therapeutic care which can help them to recover from their emotional injuries, but for these children the specialist services they require are often not available.

The next step in the SACCS story will be the establishment of a charitable trust that will underpin a college, training carers in the SACCS model. The wider implications are that this training can ultimately inform practice with traumatized children everywhere.

The Authors

Janie Rymaszewska is Deputy Director of practice development and training at SACCS with responsibility for therapy. She qualified in 1990 with a masters in creative arts in therapy from Hahnemann University Medical School, Philadelphia, and is a registered movement therapist. She has spent 20 years working with traumatized children and adolescents, with a particular interest in movement analysis, body work and the effects of traumatization on the body. She spent many years using play and movement in the NHS, working in London at Great Ormond Street Hospital for Sick Children, Maudsley Hospital, Guy's Hospital, and Kingston-upon-Thames Hospital. She has worked in private practice with autistic children, adolescent stroke victims, children with severe hearing impairment, and young people with emotional and behavioural problems. Since 2001 she has worked with severely traumatized children and young people at SACCS using movement, play and body work. She has worked as a consultant to Gertrude's Garden Children's Hospital, Nairobi, Kenya, assessing play provision with children who are HIV positive, while offering ways, through play, to reduce trauma and chronic regression due to hospitalization.

Terry Philpot is a journalist and writer and a contributor to, among others, *The Tablet* and *Times Higher Education Supplement*. He was formerly editor of *Community Care*. He has written and edited several books, the latest of which are (with Anthony Douglas) *Adoption: Changing Families, Changing Times* (2002), (with Julia Feast) *Searching Questions: Identity, Origins and Adoption* (BAAF Adoption and Fostering, 2003), (with Clive Sellick and June Thoburn) *What Works in Foster Care and Adoption?* (Barnardo's, 2004), and (with Richard Rose) *The Child's Own Story. Life Story Work with Traumatized Children* (Jessica Kingsley Publishers, 2004). He has also published reports on private fostering, kinship care, and residential care for older people run by the Catholic Church. He is a trustee of Rainer, the Centre for Policy on Ageing, and the Social Care Institute for Excellence. He is an associate of the Children and Families Research Unit, De Montfort University. He has won several awards for journalism.

Subject Index

Author Index